# COMMUNICATION CINEMA DEVELOPMENT

## From Morosity to Hope

# Communication Cinema Development

## FROM MOROSITY TO HOPE

GASTON ROBERGE

MANOHAR
2026

First published 1998
Reprinted 2026
First eBook edition 2026



ISBN 978-81-7304-149-5 (Hb)
ISBN 978-93-7451-250-0 (ebook)

*Published by*
Ajay Kumar Jain *for*
Manohar Publishers & Distributors
4753/23 Ansari Road, Daryaganj
New Delhi 110 002

Printed and bound in India

# Contents

# List of Plates

# Preface

Some time ago I saw it announced that a friend of mine was to give a public lecture entitled "from morosity to hope". That struck me as significant and timely. The phrase kept ringing in my mind. Eventually it prompted me to write the last essay of this book. Then, I realised that the essays I had written in the previous two years had been my own effort to move on from morosity to hope. For years, it had been necessary to identify the ills and evils of our world and to struggle for justice, peace, harmony, and access to the basic necessities of life for everyone on earth. The last four decades, in particular, were dominated by an ideology of development. When it became clear that development, as an international project, was not of much help to those in need, there was a grave danger for one who had been enthusiastic about "development" to lose faith in the possibility of improvement of the quality of life for everybody on earth. There was a danger of sinking in cynicism. That is why the phrase "from morosity to hope", with its inherent dynamism, was a strong inspiration as it articulated my life project at the time.

The following essays deal with three interrelated subjects: communication, cinema and development. The focus is on cinema, but cinema is always seen in the environment of communication, and it is assessed according to its contribution to development. However, both communication and development have undergone a deep change. These essays consider that change from a variety of points of view.

What is said below on development is somewhat problematic. Since the notion of development has changed and continues to change, it is necessary to ask at each step of our reflection, "what particular development are we here talking about?" Especially when very severe criticisms are levelled against development. In general, I shall talk of development seen as an international project.

Whatever you may say about development, you are likely to be caught in an argument of the type "yes, but...". If I say that there are more poor persons today than ever before, I am told, "yes, in absolute terms, but in relative terms there are less poor today than before". A fine comfort for the one billion poor people worldwide who, in most cases, live in unjust situations they cannot change!

It must be admitted, our world is not at all in good shape. I am not questioning other people's intentions. I would like to show that however praiseworthy or even necessary these intentions may be, nonetheless they do not suffice. Is it not intolerable that on the eve of the year 2000 so many people are poor, sick, homeless, countryless. These are the facts—or rather the persons—that confront us. We must try to see the limitations of the development project and we must try to create new, much more radical, projects. For that hope is required. The essays of this book would like to arise hope even in an acute awareness of our failures. Hope, after all, can have no other context.

Cinema is not an abstract notion hanging in the air. Cinema is made of the films people see, films of any kind, from the most "commercial" to the most "non-commercial". The study of the personal cinema of a great film-maker opens up a private world. The study of the most "commercial" film is, in fact, no less rewarding, as it opens up the shared world of whole groups.

Musing over my film experience has convinced me that the cinema deserves serious reflection. One wants to know how films engage him or herself. How they penetrate the recess of one's soul. How they relate to daily life. How they can tell those stories that enchant us. How they exude poetry. And beyond the "hows", there are "whys?" Why is there so much money in the movies? Why are the movies kept under such a tight control by most states? Why does everyone love movies so much? These questions are the more pressing today because cinema, confronted by television, is called upon to grow into a more mature art form.

No doubt, that "more mature" cinema may not be any more the "cinema as we have known it". Today's cinema is no more the cinema some among us, or our parents, have known in the 1930s. Yet, whatever it may be in the coming years, cinema is likely to play a capital role with regard to what we call development. Cinema will change, but its function in society, it seems to me, will endure, namely, to articulate the collective thought of a human group at a given time. Of course, cinema is not the only media to fulfil that function. But cinema is the mass media "par excellence". Television will force cinema to specialise—a gain for cinema!—in a way that is difficult to foresee because of the surprises which industrial technology always has up its sleeves.

Each of the chapters on communication (Part Two) and on cinema (Part Three) probes a particular aspect of either communication or cinema. The chapters, as a whole, do not offer a complete treatise on the subject, but they cumulatively propound a positive view, even though critical, and suggest avenues for positive action. Part Four comprises discussions of a few films. The choice of the films has been dictated by circumstances, and not by any "a priori" motive. These film discussions exemplify the type of film criticism which the theoretical reflection of the previous chapters can lead to. A film theory, it seems to me, is only as good as the criticism it makes possible. Of course, the critiques included here are not the last word on each of the films discussed. Several aspects are, of necessity, left out. But the essays, I feel, offer original considerations on films about which too little that is interesting has been written. In particular, the critiques articulate the relationship between films and "development" in specific circumstances.

A fifth part comprises one chapter only in which I compare cinema and television.

The bibliography at the end of most chapters is not offered as an exhaustive reading list on the subject dealt with in a chapter. The works mentioned list some of the readings I happened to make more or less at the time of writing this book. All of this—partial treatment of subjects, occasional film discussions, unsystematic bibliography—amply indicates that this book is not the work of a "professional" but of an "amateur" intellectual, to use Edward W. Said's useful distinction.

"The intellectual today ought to be an amateur, someone who considers that to be a thinking and concerned member of a society one is entitled to raise moral issues at the heart of even the most technical and professionalized activity as it involves one's country, its power, its mode of interacting with its citizens as well as with other societies."

## REFERENCE

Said, Edward W., *Representations of the Intellectual*, The 1993 Reith Lectures, London: Vintage, 1994, p. 61.

# Acknowledgements


Of the following 38 chapters, 37 have been published as follows:

In *Amrita Bazar Patrika*, Interface section, as a fortnightly page captioned '*Outreach*', chapters: 1, 2, 3, 4, 5, 6, 7, 8, 9, 10, 11, 13, 14, 15, 16, 17, 21, 22, 26, 27, 28, 29, 30. These essays were published between December 1993 and November 1994. I wish to thank Hashim Khairullah for persuading me to write them.

In *The Telegraph*, 6 March 1994, chapter 12.

In *West Bengal*, 10 January 1994, chapters 18, 19, 20.

In a brochure published by Nandan, the Film Centre of West Bengal, 100th Anniversary of Cinema, chapter 23.

International Film Festival of India, 10-20 January 1994, chapter 24.

In *Pratidin* (Bengali), 1 May 1994, chapter 25.

In *The Statesman*, Miscellany section, 22 August 1993, chapter 31.

In *Chalacchitram*, Dhaka, February-March 1991, pp. 15-16 (Bengali), chapter 32.

In *The Economic Times*, Calcutta, 17 November 1992, chapter 33. Bengali version in *Aajkaal*, Rabibaasar, Page "K", 31 January 1993.

In *Movie Montage*, Cine Institute, Calcutta, chapters 35, 36.

In *Chalachitrer Eksho Bachor*, Bengali rendering, chapter 37.

PART ONE

# COMMUNICATION AND DEVELOPMENT

# 1. The Need for Alternatives

Communication is the exchange of ideas and feelings among people. That exchange is always purposive. For instance, just to establish or nurture amicable relationships we exchange Christmas, Diwali or Eid greeting cards. Very little of what these greeting cards explicitly say is actually meant. Yet, we know, the exchange of greetings is essential. What we exchange has little significance but exchange we must.

At times, though, what is communicated is not that friendly. A declaration of war, for instance. In fact, not only war declarations, but all communication seeking to win someone over is warlike. This is obvious in political discourses. It may be less so in advertising. Yet, when a product or a concept is advertised worldwide, the stakes may be higher than those involved in the armed confrontation of two countries.

Without communication there would be no human life, indeed, no life at all. That is why over the years people have fought for their right to communicate. But today they are facing an entirely new situation. Recent technologies have innervated the whole world, India included, and as a result communication is now all pervasive. Unfortunately because of the manner in which it is practiced, communication often threatens the quality of human life. At the same time communication is indispensable. One is confronted, therefore, by the threat created by communication technology and the necessity of using that technology.

How does India respond to that situation? India has acceded to independent statehood somewhat recently and she is modernizing herself. That gigantic task requires all her attention and energy. But she has been suddenly caught in the communication net cast over the planet: she is addressed (aggressed?) from every side. She is forced to communicate worldwide. Signals reach her through communication networks at such a speed that time is lacking for her to consider the process. Yet, it is absolutely necessary to pause a moment in order to realise what is happening. But India is not alone to face that necessity.

For over four decades communication has been linked with so-called development. Development, whatever claims to the contrary, has always been viewed mainly as an economic project. True, the concept has evolved, but always the economic aspect has dominated. The contemporary human animal is a "homo economicus", a type of person whose supreme value is economic. But if the concept of development evolved, so did the concept of communication. Early in the development era, say, around 1950-60, one talked of a "trickle down" theory of development which held that wealth would percolate the social pyramid down to the poorest of the poor. Such a notion of development conjured a "hypodermic theory" of communication according to which messages are implanted into society, as if communicators stood outside of society and were immuned to its influence. Later, the development ideology created its companion, namely, "development communication". Development programmes were then seen as depending largely on successful dissemination of information. Later still, when emphasis was put on people"s participation in the development process, communication was called upon to "persuade" the target groups to take part whole-heartedly in the programmes so benevolently designed for them.

The target groups soon realised that development is a mirage, and development communication a ploy. Development programmes hardly ever benefit the poor, that is, the persons who need development most. So, at first, the poor looked for alternative developments. But they finally saw that development is not for them. Development is meant to consolidate a system benefiting those who already have the better share of the world's wealth. Now, the poor look for alternatives *to* development. And any alternative to development calls for alternatives to communication, especially to the institutions of communication.

The great institutions which are supposed to serve the needs of every citizen seem unable to do so. For instance, our national television network has been commercialised. A typical example of development, the economic aspect having been given the main consideration. Who then will cater to the educational and cultural needs of the country? Shall we entrust the education of our children and the cultures of our people to commercial television? We shouldn't, if we value both education and culture. For, commerce has its own laws, and these laws have little regard for values except economic values. Unless both our educational system and our national television function relatively free of commerce, they will be unable to serve the needs of the country, and people will be forced to seek alternatives. People will be forced to bypass the present institutions of education and of communication, as well as those of medicine, law enforcement, electoral system and justice. People will not need to attack these institutions, simply they will have to do for themselves what these institutions do not do for them.

Those who have the power of money and office have established themselves at the centre of peoples' lives. The minority has marginalised the majority. A new education will help the people of the majority to realise that they are the centre, and the institutions that do not serve their needs are to be marginalised. As it is, the majority of the people have to struggle in order to survive. The new education should further enable them to do so. This surely is not an easy task. For, the present economic centre needs large, indigent and dependent, margins. But by failing to provide them with their basic needs the centre is forcing the margins to become "dangerously" independent.

Independence from the great institutions has today become a necessity. Unfortunately, such independence exacerbates the present crisis in governability, increases internal tension and delays the creation of those institutions that are required in any society. For, institutions are a uniquely human form of organisation. They make social life harmonious and fruitful. But the twin option for democracy and free market strait-jackets the institutions of society.

The laws of the free-market and the laws of democracy are expected to concur in distributing wealth and power among all. But, in practice, they gather power and wealth in the hands of the few. That is because the power of office acquired democratically enables those who have it to favour the market. For instance, people do not get jobs now, not for lack of training, but because at the moment the market does not need more workers. But what is the priority, market or workers? Policies set by democratically elected leaders suggest that the market has been made the sole master of human life—a god of sorts, Mammon.

We are told that the Incas used to sacrifice human beings to their gods. The Incas believed that they thus pleased the gods and that the latter would maintain the established order. We are not told whether the victims were happy about their fate, but we can assume that the priestly class was happy about its own fate. Today millions of workers, men, women and even children, are sacrificed to the market. In that way, it is hoped, the system will function well. The victims are, at first, recalcitrant, but they soon accept their fate. As for the ruling classes they easily convince themselves that the sacrifices are inevitable (especially when suffered by others). And few people imagine that the world could be organised in a different way. For. our minds and hearts have been quite successfully colonised by the ideology of the free market. Yet, to imagine other and better worlds and to strive to bring them about, that is hope.

## REFERENCES

Swami Agnivesh: "We have explored all the legal avenues for the last 15 years and are convinced that it is impossible for the judiciary to act as a redressal forum for these hapless people." *The Statesman*, 21 March 1994, front page.

Alvares, Claude, "The Violence of Development", in *Twin Features*, Goa, March 1993.

Esteva, Gustavo, "A New Source of Hope: The Margins", in *Interculture*, Vol. xxvi, No. 2, Spring 1993, Issue No. 119.

Hamelink, Cees, "Information Super-Highway: Quo Vadis?" in *IDOC Internazionale*, 95:4, October-December, pp. 5-9.

Kohli, Atul, "Democracy amid economic orthodoxy: trends in developing countries", in *Third World Quarterly*, Journal of Emerging Areas, Vol. 14, No. 4, November 1993, pp. 671-89.

"at least over the last decade, international pressures and new middle class elites within these (developing) countries have colluded to pursue highly inegalitarian economic strategies in the name of market rationality, further contributing to dissatisfaction and governability problems", pp. 671-2.

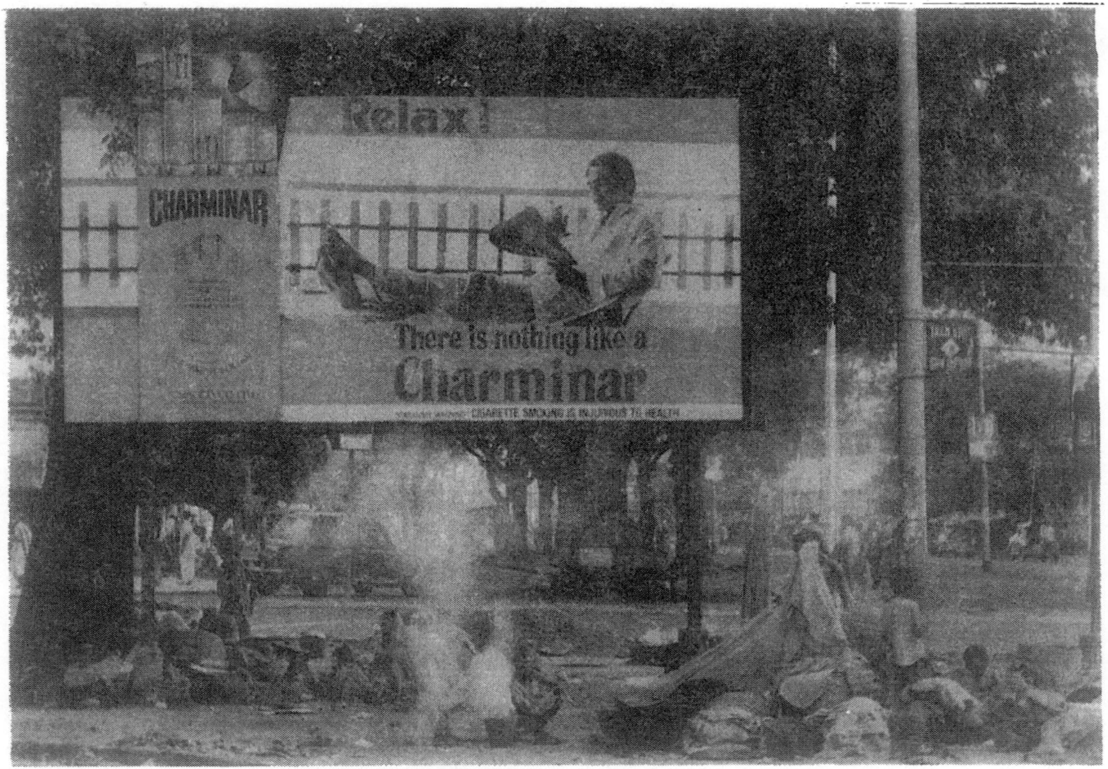


1. The poor have soon understood that development was a mirage.
Salim Paul

# PART TWO

# COMMUNICATION

# 2. Communication is for Communion

Can we talk about communication? Of course, we can. And indeed we should. Why?

As the word 'communication' suggests, we communicate in order to share and to become one. But although a lot of communication takes place, the goal of communication, namely, communion, is rarely achieved.

Talking about communication? Everybody likes to believe that he or she knows everything about it. For, everybody communicates. So what is there to say about it which one might not know?

Well, it's not a matter of knowing something so much as it is a matter of being aware of something. And what one has to be aware of is that communication occurs in more ways than in the exchange of words, spoken or written. Yet, we mistakenly locate communication mostly in the exchange of words.

Take, for instance, this text which you read. You will have noticed—or have you?—that the text is broken into small units. Some breathing space is created between the units. That spacing is communication too. That way the text is modulated. If I were to read my text aloud I could add more modulations still.

Modulation of a text is communication. At times more important than the text itself. And that is the main point. Remember the last time—not too far back, I hope—when you were told, "I love you". Was not the modulation, that is, the tone of the voice, the smile, perhaps, all important? Indeed, was not modulation the message?

Sometimes we hear people complaining, "so and so told me this or that, I could take it, but the way he said it, that I could not swallow". That is just it. The way something is said is part of the message, it is communication.

We can and should go one step further. Not only is the way a thing is said often more important than the thing said, but moreover, at times the thing said is not even meant.

I am not referring to lies, of course, but to "ways of saying". For instance, when you ask a person "how are you?" you do not expect the person to actually tell you how he or she is. Indeed, it's somewhat embarrassing when to the question "how are you?" one begins a long description of one's state of health, of one's last sleepless night, or of a nagging headache.

Then, why should I ask anyone "how are you?" if I do not mean to be told how that one is? The point is "how are you?" (except in the mouth of a doctor, perhaps) means, "I care for you—to an extent".

Any one who learns a foreign language comes across these strange but common phrases that are not meant. For instance, in American English, if one says "I'll see you", one does not expect to be asked "when?" "I'll see you" means just "let us keep our relationship open".

Similarly, in Bengali when one asks a person "where are you going?" one does not usually expect to be told accurately where that person is going. Or, again in Bengali, "come" may mean "go away". For instance, after a stormy encounter and verbal battle with his opponent a person might say, in Bengali, of course, "you may *come* now".

On the one hand, the modulation of the message is as important as the so-called message itself. On the other hand, the so-called message itself often is not meant. These simple observations enlighten us on the nature of communication. Namely, communication has to do with sharing of feelings perhaps more than it has to do with sharing of ideas.

Unfortunately, this overly pragmatic world of ours tries to give more importance to the sharing of ideas than to the sharing of feelings. Indeed, since communication is for communion, it does not consist mainly in what is said, but in the feelings that are shared. We communicate in order to keep bound with others in friendly relationships.

For the last few centuries, however, our world has given more attention to ideas, to rational processes in communication. It is not surprising, therefore, to find that students of cinema or television often go merely for content analysis, reducing the content of a programme or of a film to the explicit words that can be heard or that are seen written.

This approach, especially in the case of television, is catastrophic. For it leaves out the modulation, the "way" things are said, the visuals that give a context to the text. In other words, this approach leaves out most of the intended message and concentrates on what is said in words.

Today we are learning to live with the medium of television. TV is a new medium of communication for most viewers in India. Moreover, the programme-makers have started to use more fully the potential of the television medium to modulate their messages, to use "ways" of putting things across.

Perhaps now, more than ever before, we face the necessity of learning about communication. For, we are surrounded by a new communication environment. And if we can judge by the crores of rupees spent on television we can rest assured that television is assumed to be able to communicate and is used to communicate.

But we, as viewers, need not be passive recipients of this pervasive communication. We can come to understand it and even to answer it back. In a real way, though not quite the way one answers a phone call. But then, what would one answer if one was asked by one's television set "how are you?" The fact is, one is constantly addressed by one's TV set.

If my friends greet me with a "how are you?" I know what they mean, and I know what to answer. The question facing us now is, what can television actually mean in whatever it tells us? Ought we not to know? For, television addresses us constantly, and aggresses us too often.

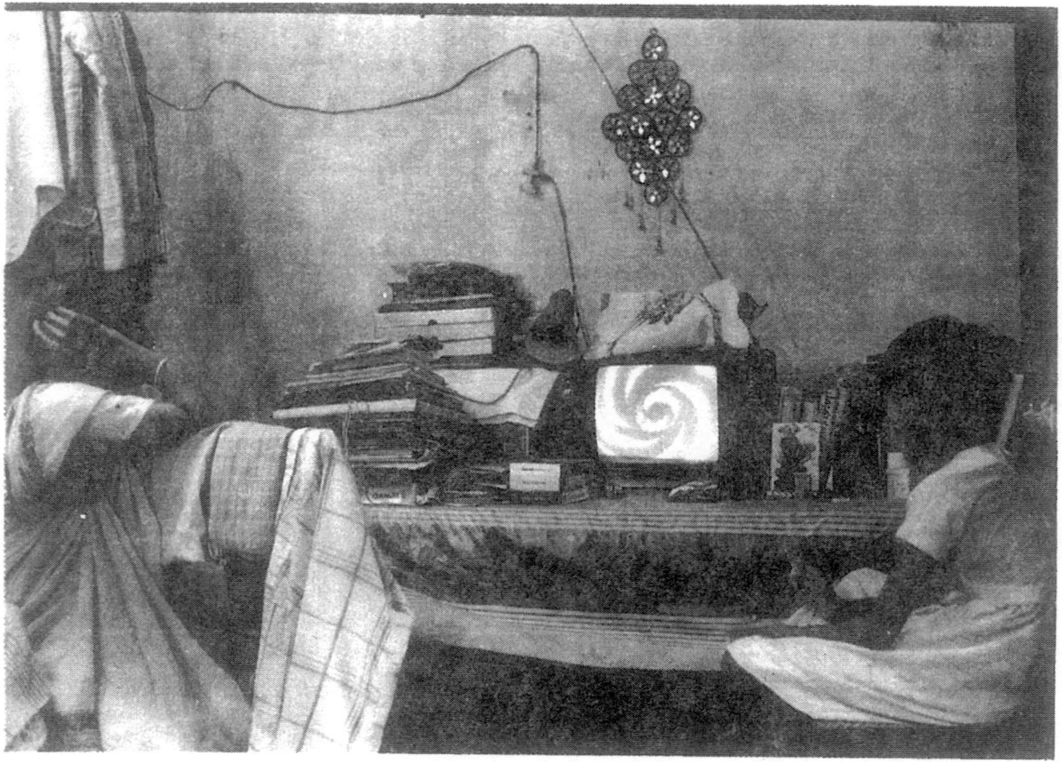

2. Television addresses us constantly, and aggresses us too often.
P.B. Chaki

# 3. The Right to Communicate

The ancient human race should have learnt by now to live in harmony within itself and with its environment. But, alas, that is not the case. In the last three or four centuries, in the West especially and in those countries the West influenced, the relationship of "man" with "nature" has been one of opposition. What was just a logical distinction between man and his environment has been made into a real opposition. For, obviously, there can be no actual separation of humans from their environment. They breathe the ambient air, they receive light and heat from the sun, they respond to gravitational attraction, they eat the produce of the earth and, in time, they return to dust. Where would you draw the line, if a line could be drawn, between a human being and its environment? Humans are integral parts of nature, the so-called environment.

But as the West industrialised an exploitative relationship developed between people and nature. Infinite resources were required to sustain industrialisation and the urbanisation it made necessary. And "man" plundered the earth. A suitable ideology was created to legitimise that exploitation. The ideology had its different ramifications, in biology (the then dominant science), for instance, with its "survival of the fittest" doctrine, and above all in religion with the supposedly Biblical injunction of "dominating the world".

The split between "man" and "nature" had its counterpart between man and man. Some humans were construed to be the environment of "man" and thus they could be exploited: women, children, non-white people, workers of all races. However, since all humans are equal and since they know it, humans have constantly resisted this exploitation, even if with limited success. (Nature, though more pliable, has its own protection mechanisms, and it is always victorious in the end. For, to take the most extreme case of aggression against "nature", whom would "man" actually destroy if "he" destroyed the planet?)

Given the social nature of humans, it is not surprising that the struggle to resist aggression, oppression, marginalisations of all sorts, takes place to a large extent in the arena of communication. For, communication always articulates power. Those who wield power easily believe that resistance must be silenced, and that thoughts must be controlled. For, in their view, it is not enough to contain resistance, the very thought of resistance must be countered, better still, annihilated. The extent, the sophistication, the violence of communication control is a cause for wonder. How can humans employ their minds to inflict such violence onto other humans, the flesh of their flesh, is beyond comprehension.

It is mostly since the 1970s onward that worldwide attention has been given to communication. In recognition of this increased awareness the year 1983 was declared the International Year of Communication. Never before had so much concern been aroused by communication. In fact, the international community had to address the changes in communication which resulted from the advent of electronic and satellite technology. New problems arose. These are such that our forefathers could hardly anticipate them, and they are so complex that some people today are not even aware that their development, perhaps even their survival, depends on the solution given to these problems.

This awareness of communication is not only academic. It implies fundamental rights, designated in a summative manner as the *right to communicate*. The awareness of this right is ancient. This writer, unfortunately, can trace its history solely in terms of the West. There, people discussing face to face on the Greek "agora" or the Roman "forum" experienced their *right to opinion*. But it is much later, in the fifteen century, with the invention of the printing press, that the *freedom of expression* became an issue. That freedom had to be conquered from and preserved against both the civil and the religious authorities. Earlier on, iconographers making religious images had to accept the prescriptions of the religious authorities on their art.

In the nineteenth century the press had to constantly struggle to acquire and preserve *the freedom of the press*. The subsequent development of the other mass media and their vast use and abuse demonstrated the need for and the possibility of the right "to seek, receive and impart information and ideas through any media regardless of frontiers" (Article 19, Universal Declaration of Human Rights, 1948).

Today the consciousness of the right to communicate is progressing, though not without difficulty and opposition. The right to communicate comprises several rights, like: a right to assemble, to discuss, to participate and related *association rights*; a right to inquire, to be informed, to inform and related *information rights*; a right to culture, to choose, to privacy and related human *development rights*.

Rights are hardly ever given. Either one already enjoys them or, more frequently one has to wrestle them out of the clutches of others. That is why, rights always connote a context of struggle and too often, to fuel the struggle, of hatred. Sustained efforts are deployed to conscientize "oppressed" people about their rights. That is necessary. But too little, it seems to me, is done to conscientize people about the rights of others and about the necessity to respect these rights, if not quite out of love and compassion, at least in a calculated understanding of one's long term survival.

From the early 1970s onward, the need for a new World Information and Communication Order was widely discussed and this resulted in the formulation in 1976 of a Declaration by a group of countries, spelling out the imbalances (in plain language, the injustices) then prevalent and their proposed remedies. The United States of America strongly opposed that Declaration because, they argued, it endangered the "free flow" of information, a doctrine to which the USA are committed. In 1985 the USA withdrew from the UNESCO, followed by UK the next year. On a global level efforts at promoting the right of communication for all had been defeated.

The doctrine of the "free" flow of information had triumphed, and soon after the reality of the "free" market materialised in all its might.

## REFERENCES

Harms, L.S., "An Emergent Communication Policy Science: Content, Rights, Problems and Methods", Honolulu, Department of Communication, University of Hawaii, quoted in MacBride, p. 173.

Macbride, Sean *et al.*, *Many Voices, One World. Communication and Society, Today and Tomorrow,* Report by the International Commission for the Study of Communication Problems, "Towards a new more just and more efficient world information and communication order", UNESCO, 1980.

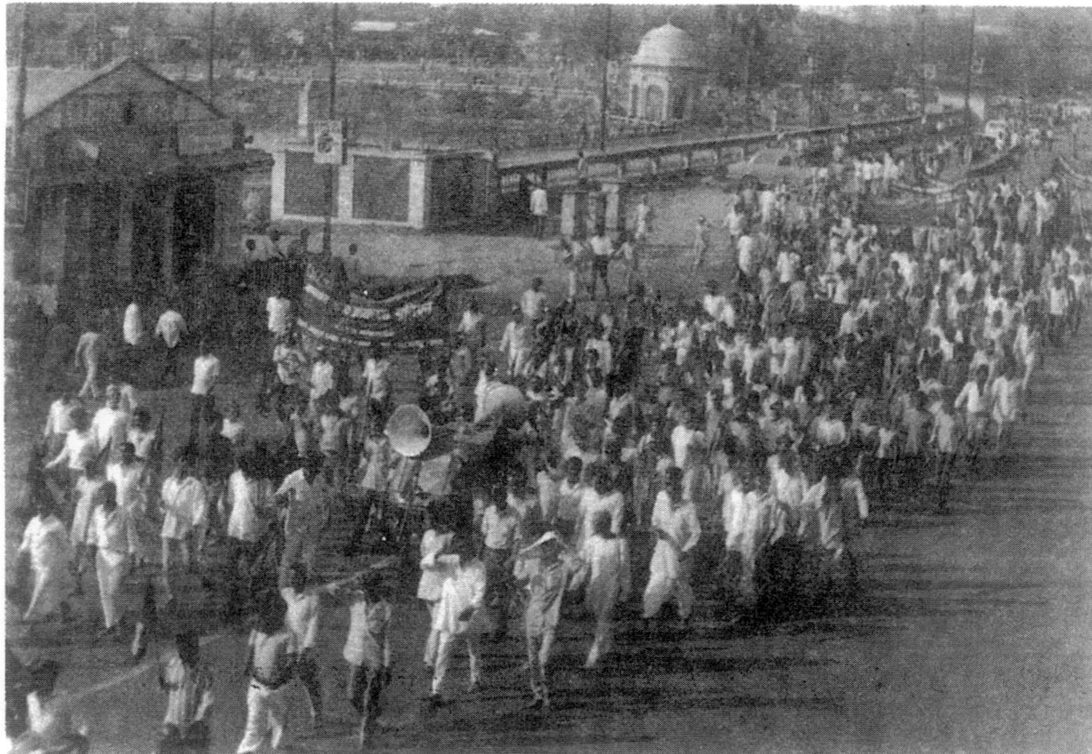

3. Rights are hardly ever given. Either one already enjoys them or, more frequently, one has the wrestle them out of the clutches of others.
Dev Kumar Nayak

# 4. WHO says WHAT to WHOM in what CHANNEL with what EFFECT?—And So?

Communication is so complex a phenomenon that no one approach or theory can exhaust the subject. Various approaches have been explored.

The theoreticians of communication in the late 1940s were concerned with the exchange of messages. Many of these theoreticians were mathematicians. So, they formulated theories in which the exchange of messages could be measured, and the efficiency of the process could be assessed. One of these theoreticians held that in order to deal adequately with a communication process, you have to examine it in the fivefold aspect of "*who* says *what* to *whom* in what *channel* with what *effect*?"

The neat formula looked very thorough then. Examining these five aspects of communication, one had the feeling that one had exhausted the subject, one had come to know all that there was to know. But there are still many aspects of communication which the fivefold question does not touch. The formula also looked very novel. But in fact, it was a rehash of Aristotle's five causes: efficient, material, formal, exemplary and final. Forensic experts too have long had a maxim of Aristotelian parentage. It was coined when people still used Latin, "who, what, when, with whose help, why, how, when?" (*quis, quid, ubi, quibus auxiliis, cur, quomodo, quando*?). So, the fivefold question raised by communication experts was not so new, after all. Nevertheless their approach is still indispensable today when the flow of communication messages has increased immensely and, of course, continues to increase.

Yet, in time other concerns emerged. One of these is meaning. For the manager of a telephone company it is enough to know that the messages carried by the company reach their destinations efficiently and economically. But how are these messages understood? How is meaning conveyed by a message, and how is meaning grasped by the recipient? These questions have to do with immaterial elements, several of which can hardly be measured or even anticipated. For instance, how complex can an advertising message be, given the environment in which it will be received, say, between two segments of a televised tennis match? How long can the repetition of a message about family planning, for instance, be useful before it generates boredom and even antagonism?

There are yet other aspects of communication that require attention. Power, for instance. Whenever communication occurs, a power structure is implied, articulated and most often strengthened. When you address an officer as "sir", you acknowledge that at least as far as his office is concerned the officer deserves your respect or, in other words, the officer is in a position of superiority over you.

The very words that you use position you within a relationship. In Bengali, for instance, you have different forms of address—*apni, tumi, tui* all three meaning "you", but each one being indicative of the particular relationship between two persons. For example, in the late Satyajit Ray's film, *Ghare Baire* (*The Home and the World*), when Bimala falls in love with her relative, she shifts at one moment of emotional involvement from the more formal *apni* to the more familiar *tumi*. But almost immediately, conscious of her lapse, she reverts to *apni*. In an English translation this finesse of the language is lost, whereas the French rendering with its *vous* and *tu* adequately renders the dramatic evolution of the amorous relationship.

Yet another important aspect of communication has to do with the aura of meaning that surrounds a word. That is, the aura of "connotation" and of symbolism. Each word we use seems to have a fixed meaning since that meaning is given in a dictionary. But that is a short term view of the matter. In fact, the meaning of a word keeps changing over time. That is why dictionaries are really historical listings of each word's meanings.

But in addition to this shifting in time, the meaning of a word is enriched by association with events, with other words, with popular ideas. Some of these associations stick to the word and are activated whenever the word is used. Take for instance, the word "development". Since the 1940s it has been loaded with a plus value. Development projects, up to the late 1980s, were seen in a positive light. Strangely, throughout these four decades, the actual meaning of the word "development" remained floating, polarised by "economic", on the one hand, and "humane", on the other hand. You could pull the meaning one side or the other. But then, after four decades of development schemes, it became evident that the humane was most often at odds with the economic. The economic always had the upper hand.

Most often the word "development" appeared in contexts of either science, technology, power and specialization, on the one hand, or, on the other hand, of fulfilment, growth and actualisation of potential. These concepts became so strongly associated with that of development, that the use of the latter term caused these other concepts to vibrate, as if in harmony, and to add their various significations to the term development. And thus, development came to be seen as a scientific process to be directed by specialists. Given the right "inputs" the process would deliver the expected "outputs". But we have now realised that stripped of its scientific cloak, "official" development is the development of the prevalent economic system. Whatever the human cost.

Any one using language is caught in a net. Words permit one to say things, but only certain things and always with the implication of certain other things. Without language you could not think and speak at all, but with a specific language, and there are only specific languages, you are determined to think and express specific thoughts in specific ways. Thinking is really to cope with this problem more or less successfully.

In more than one sense, you need to "watch your language". Watching one's language is not only a matter of propriety. It is a matter of wisdom. We may have the impression that we control language. But that is an illusion. In more than one way language leads us. That is why it is so important to develop theories which permit us to understand the phenomenon of language in communication. But, alas, theories too are couched in words. Thus, we never quite escape the net of language. Yet, we none the less succeed in having ourselves understood, more still, we do understand others and enter into communion with them. To carry on communicating in spite of all obstacles, is, of course, hope.

## REFERENCE

Rosenthal, Peggy, *Words and Values: Some Leading Words and Where They Lead Us*, Oxford: Oxford University Press, 1984. See Part Two, "Growth and Development to Realize Your Potential", pp. 47-111.

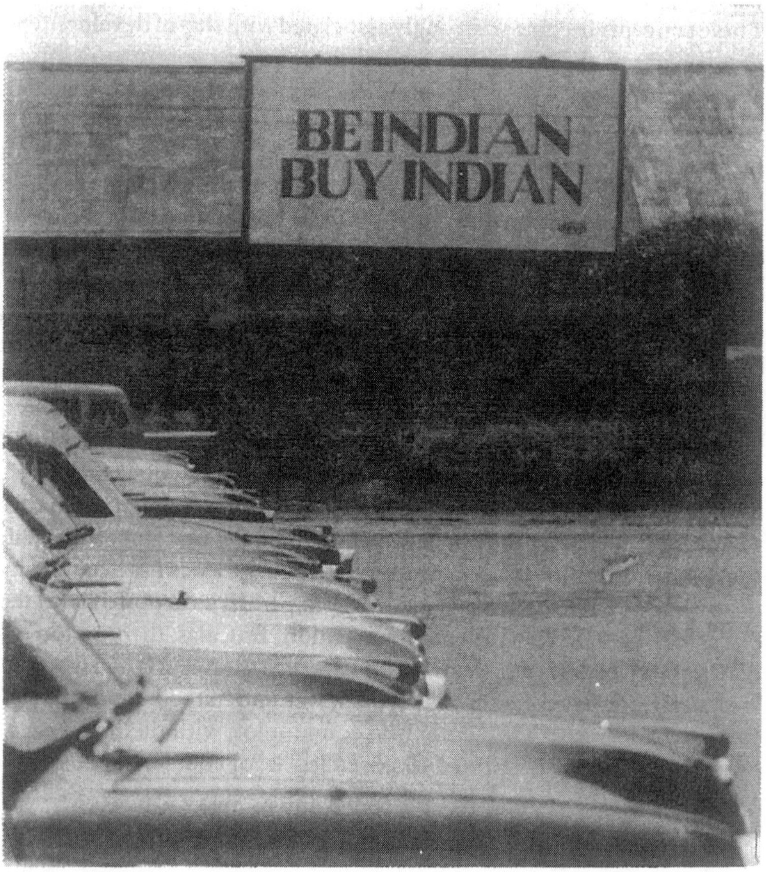


4. The flow of communication messages has increased immensely and, of course, continues to increase.
Salim Paul

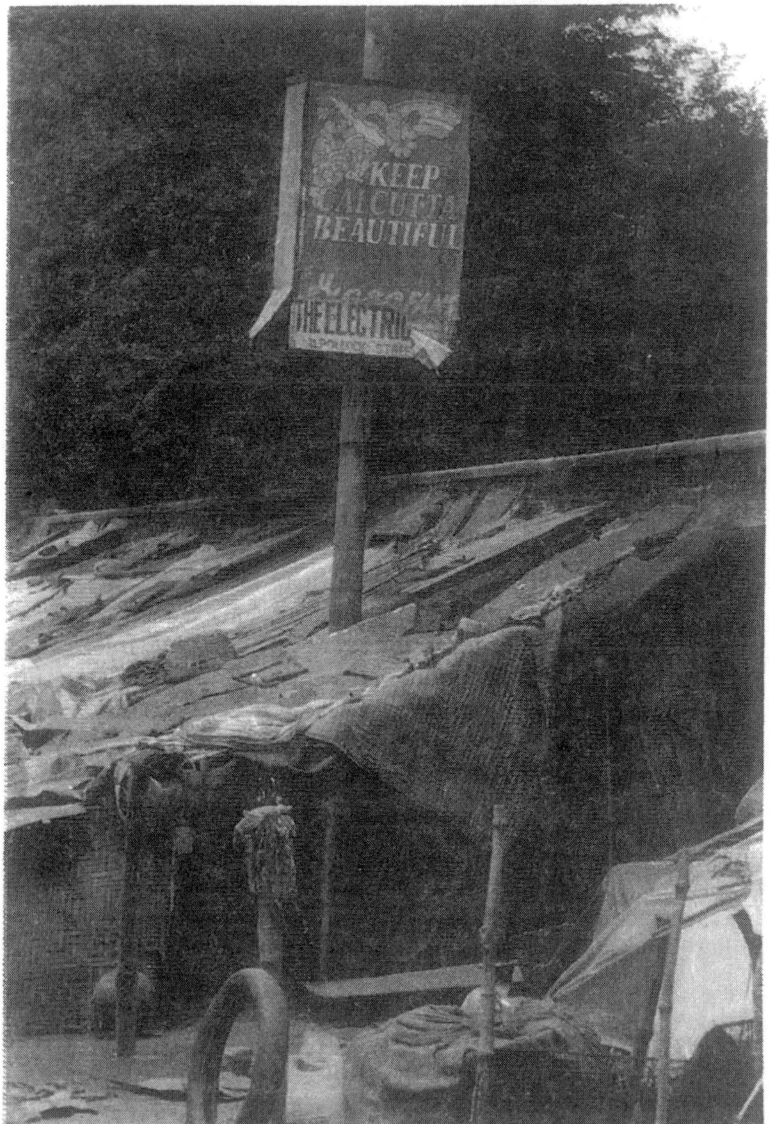


5. How long can the repetition of a message be useful before it generates boredom and even antagonism?
Salim Paul

# 5. Universal Education Died under Friendly Fire

How is it possible for some of us to confuse education and literacy? Education is a state of mind, literacy is a technological skill. You need both education and literacy in order to function in society. But literacy does not make you educated. On the other hand, you can be quite educated and have no literacy or numeracy skills.

Not only have we equated literacy with education, but we have equated education itself with formal courses of studies. We say that Prof. X was educated at Harvard University, for example. Thus, we take literacy to be the first step towards being educated, followed by graduated stages of formal schooling. Sad to say, neither literacy nor schooling, as we have them now, can be said to be education.

Then what is education?

The Delhi Declaration of December 1993 on Education, signed by the heads of nine so-called "high population developing countries" (Bangladesh, Brazil, China, Egypt, India, Indonesia, Mexico, Nigeria and Pakistan), states that

> education is the pre-eminent means for promoting universal human values, the quality of human resources, and respect for cultural diversity (Article 2.2).

and

> the content and methods of education must be developed to serve the basic learning needs of individuals and societies, to empower them to address their most pressing problems—combating poverty, raising productivity, improving living conditions, and protecting the environment—and to enable them to play their rightful role in building democratic societies and enriching cultural heritage (Article 2.4).

Education, we are told will be universal by the year 2000! But with the runaway human population growth, and the disproportionate expenditures in favour of higher education, the goal of universal basic education has become quite elusive. Yet, the Declaration affirms that its signatories are committed to work towards the "the goal of education for all by the year 2000" or, a wise provision, "at the earliest possible moment".

It is only in 1986 that the Government of India has admitted that the school would not reach all children, especially millions of girls and working children, and hence India's national policy called for a systematic programme of Non-Formal Education to universalise education. Meanwhile, already in 1975 with the Satellite Instructional Television Experiment (SITE) and in 1983 with the COUNTRYWIDE CLASSROOM, India has started to use television for mass education. The COUNTRYWIDE CLASSROOM, for instance, is telecast seven days a week and offers higher education programmes to the undergraduate students of India's 7500 colleges. An estimated audience of twenty lakhs watch regularly the "UGC Programmes", as the COUNTRYWIDE CLASSROOM is popularly called. This means that not a few people throughout India want to acquire education. Yet, Doordarshan has had to cancel the UGC programmes several times to accommodate sports events. Doordarshan was created for the primary purpose of serving the educational needs of India. But the promotion of the market economy in India is forcing Doordarshan to go commercial, and the organisation is left with very little educational zeal.

Commercial television enterprises are planning to create educational television channels in Asia. If the USA (not the UK, for a change) must be our model, then let us look at what is happening there. Some American public schools are closing down, and wherever that happens education is taken over by commercial firms. These companies claim that they will buy, sell and deliver education as a commodity like no system did in the past. So, why should they not make money in the process? Education for profit. Since the sixties we have been used to "advertorials" (advertising in newspapers camouflaged as editorial). Now we have TV "infotainment" and "docutainment". Anything, so long as it sells and entertains.

According to newspaper reports, the firm Burger King has opened Burger Academies in a number of US cities, and Whittle Communications has contracted over 10,000 schools with nearly 8 million pupils. Daily these children are to see 12 minutes of commercials for chocolates and fast foods. In return, their school gets on loan a dish antenna and a TV set for each of its classrooms. In India, a good percentage of school-going children attend private schools. Thus, a discrimination is already taking place in favour of the more fortunate. With further privatisation and commercialisation of education, it can be expected that not only universal education will not occur by the year 2000 but the exact opposite will take place. By the year 2000 and thereafter education in India will be less and less universal.

On the other hand, the poor will not derive any benefit from acquiring literacy and numeracy unless they at the same time are educated on the lines described by the Declaration quoted above. It is imperative that every means should be mobilised to give our children the minimum education, including literacy, which they have the right to receive: mass media like television (for instance, the COUNTRYWIDE CLASSROOM), radio (state owned or private), audio and video cassettes, schools for street children, community centres, panchayats, night schools, theatre groups have to be mobilised.

But one thing is sure: if the masses receive the education envisaged in the Declaration, then they will be "empowered to address their most pressing problems", and they will be enabled "to play their role in building more democratic societies". The question is: do we wish the masses to be thus empowered and enabled? There is every indication that we hardly wish it. For, needy educated persons can be "troublesome". They may demand changes quite different from those advocated by the IMF (no, not "International Mammonish Fun" but "International Monetary Fund"). "Adjustments" have been made under the name of "development" over the last four decades. Yet, the number of the poor, the sick and the illiterate has grown worldwide. From 1980 onward the IMF has called for considerable reduction of the funds for education. Countries undergoing intense so-called "structural-adjustments" have had to decrease their government expenditures on education by as much as 15 per cent. And inflation has further reduced whatever was left. The goal of the Declaration has already been hit to death by friendly-fire. Or is it that we are in a state of war, facing enemies?

## REFERENCES

*The Delhi Declaration*, 16 December 1993, Education for All Summit.

*Education for All: The Indian Scene*, Department of Education, Ministry of Human Resource Development, Government of India, December 1993.

The New Internationalist, No. 248, October 1993. *Back to the Drawing Board. The War on Education.* Passim.

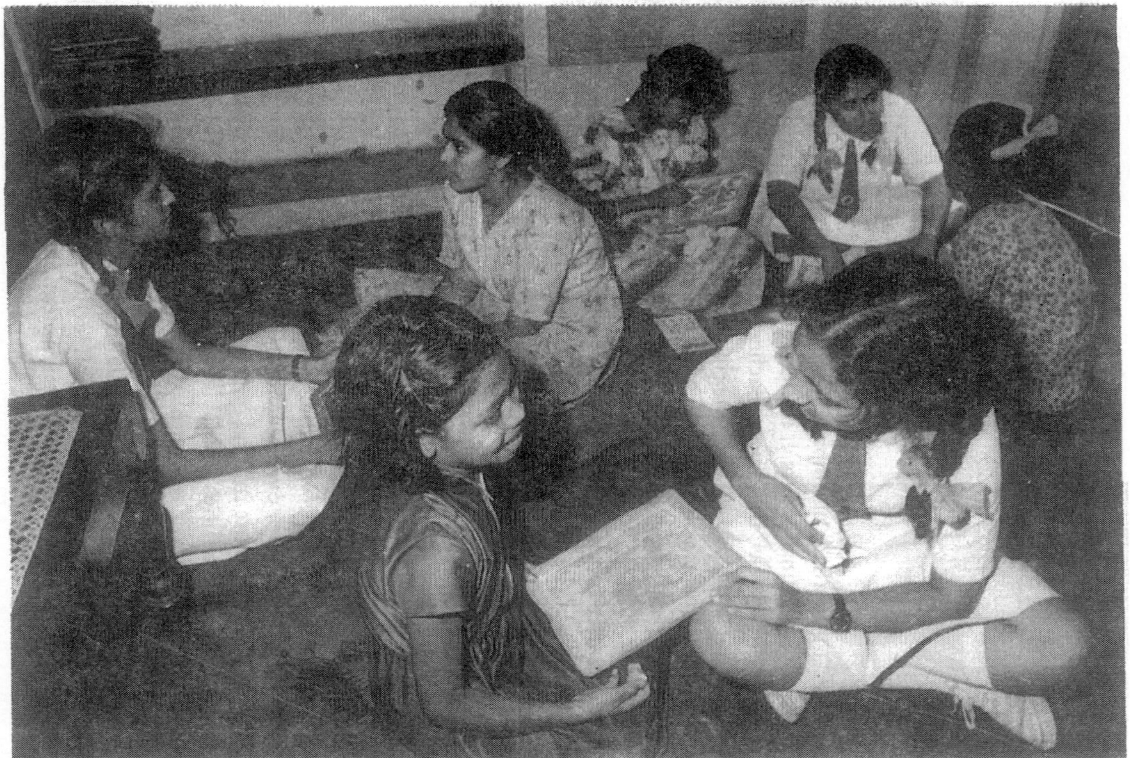

6. Teaching street children, for these Calcutta school girls, part of their own education.
Salim Paul

# 6. A Classroom Countrywide

The present method of imparting education through schools and colleges is grossly inadequate. It could be improved: build more schools, print more textbooks, train more teachers. This might appear to be the most appropriate approach. India has human resources. And an increase in the number of teaching posts would provide useful employment to more of our people.

In a way, that is what India has been trying to do for decades, especially since Independence. But the fast increase in population and the advances in the various fields of science constantly enlarging the scope of the syllabi, have rendered India unable to offer adequate education to all.

In these circumstances might not television be a way of complementing the educational system? Yes, and India has taken that option. We shall examine its working with regard to colleges. In 1983 the University Grants Commission created a television COUNTRYWIDE CLASSROOM, with programmes designed for undergraduate college students. There are nearly 7,500 colleges in India. Not all of them have the required libraries, laboratories or even teachers. Furthermore, since more than half of these colleges are in rural or semi-urban areas they do not have access to all the facilities available in cities. The COUNTRYWIDE CLASSROOM is meant to complement the teaching given in these colleges.

It may seem that a certain loss of faith in our human resources has prompted that choice in favour of high technology. But that is not the case. For, if there is an awareness of the potential of technology to reach out to the whole of India in a minimum of time and at a relatively low cost, there also is an unshakable confidence that the academic community is able to create the educational programmes for telecast as COUNTRYWIDE CLASSROOM by the national network.

Since 1983 seventeen production centres (see map) have been created under as many universities, and in 1994 no less than 3000 programmes of higher education had been produced by these centres and telecast throughout India. The programmes could have been produced by only one centre: but it was felt that in order to draw from the cultural variety of the country and, above all, in order to make it possible to as many teachers as possible to contribute programmes, at least one production centre should be created, if possible, in each state.

The Consortium for Educational Communication, a registered society, has been set up in Delhi to coordinate, on behalf of the University Grants Commission, the work of the centres. Each centre, according to its size and capability, is expected to produce each month from three to nine programmes of 20 minutes—not a minor task. In practice, any one producer in those centres is expected to produce two programmes monthly. Each centre is called Audio Visual Research Centre (AVRC) or Educational Media Research Centre (EMRC), depending on its size. All AVRCs and EMRCs are equipped with some of the best television equipment available, namely, Betacam. Thus, in hardly ten years the UGC has created one of the largest educational television production agency in the world.

A survey conducted by a professional commercial organisation, involving 15,000 telespectators in 27 Indian cities, has revealed that nearly 200 lakhs people watch the UGC programmes occasionally. Nearly 120 lakhs watch at least once a week. Some 70 lakhs watch 3 to 5 times a week. And 8 lakhs people watch daily.

From the beginning English has been used for all the programmes of the COUNTRYWIDE CLASSROOM. Naturally, the suggestion has come repeatedly that the programmes should be in regional languages. A reasonable suggestion. Indeed, some of the UGC programmes are now telecast in Hindi, and there are plans to produce programmes in other languages too in addition to English. There is no question of discontinuing English for the time being. But once Hindi and other regional languages are used, will English be retained?

However, the following points may be considered. First, the production of programmes in diverse regional languages strains our production resources. Should we not concentrate on making more and better programmes in one language, only, namely, English? Second, since only a few of the main languages will be used, some of the weaker sections of our population will never have programmes in their languages. Is not English more useful to them? Third, students are educated in their mother tongues, and the UGC programmes are only a complement to that education. It can be argued, therefore, that it would be a considerable advantage to the students if all the UGC programmes were in English only. The students would thus have the chance to learn the English vocabulary and phrases used in their disciplines. With little effort they would gain access to a whole literature available only in English. Unfortunately, thinking about languages tends to be influenced by nationalistic sentiments and perhaps by a certain intellectual laziness. Let me not be misunderstood: I am not saying that all teaching should be in English. I am saying that the supplementary teaching offered by the COUNTRYWIDE CLASSROOM should be in English only.

The national television is in a period of rapid expansion and it is not yet clear at what time the UGC programmes will finally be telecast. It has been suggested that the UGC programmes should be telecast outside class hours, when the students are free. This makes sense only because at the moment hardly any college has succeeded in integrating the UGC programmes within its time table. But, in fact, watching of the programmes by the students should be organised during class hours in each college. For this, in each college there should be a particular classroom available for watching the programmes. One staff member, having studied the schedule of programmes for the month ahead, would inform the teachers about these programmes and invite specific groups of students to come, at the time of telecast, to watch programmes that relate to the subject these students are being taught at the time. Of course, to thus prepare both teachers and students, the colleges should receive some notes on each programme along with the schedule. It may take yet some time before such notes can be sent in advance to the colleges.

The COUNTRYWIDE CLASSROOM provides a good example of the problems created in any society by the introduction of new communication technologies. This is a time when people criticise the quality of some of the programmes offered by Doordarshan. Yet, Doordarshan does telecast the UGC COUNTRYWIDE CLASSROOM of which everyone can be proud. But, for whatever reasons, the colleges do not make arrangements for their students to see these programmes, and thus the objective of the COUNTRYWIDE CLASSROOM cannot be fully achieved. On the other hand, the language in which the programmes are made shows how the induction of technology can have political implications.

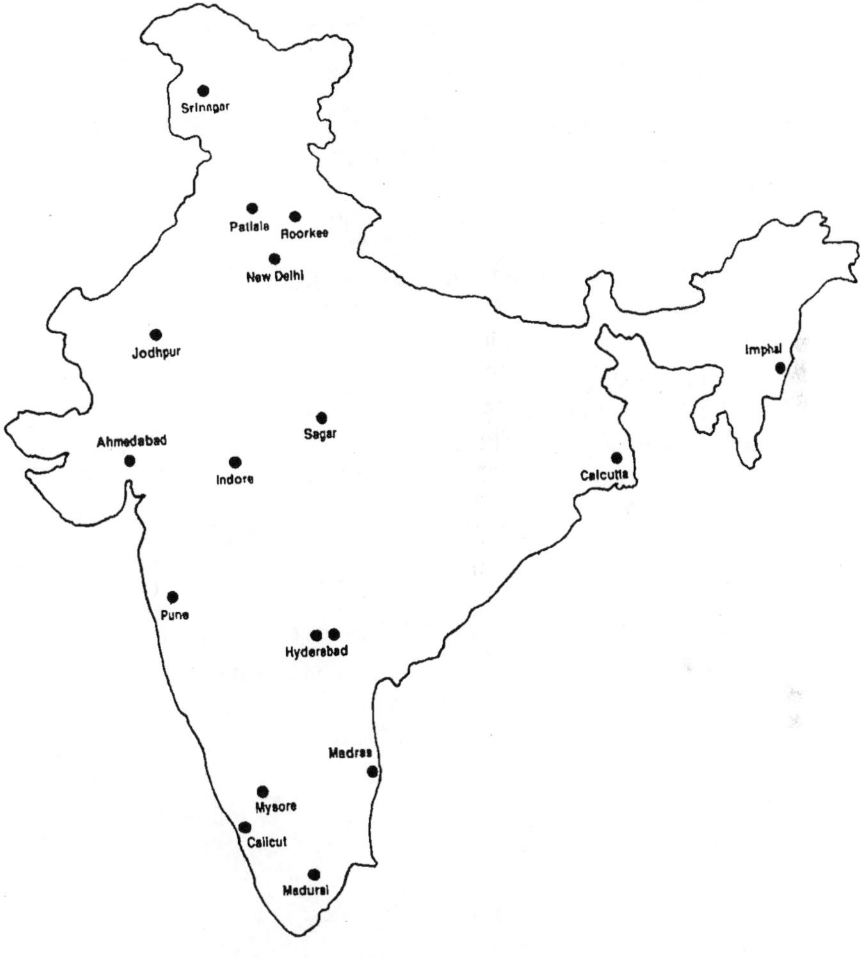


The external boundaries of India depicted in this map are neither correct nor authentic

MAP OF INDIA

*UGC Production Centres (As of March 1996)*

Ahmedabad, Gujarat University, EMRC
Calcutta, St. Xavier's College, Calcutta University, EMRC
Calicut, Calicut University, AVRC
New Delhi, Jamia Millia Islamia, EMRC
Hyderabad, Central Institute of English and Foreign Languages, EMRC
Hyderabad, Osmania University, AVRC
Imphal, Manipur University, AVRC
Indore, Devi Ahilya Vishwavidyalaya, EMRC
Jodhpur, Jai Narain Vyas University, EMRC
Madras, Anna University of Technology, AVRC
Madurai, Madurai Kamaraj University, EMRC
Mysore, University of Mysore, AVRC
Patiala, Punjabi University, AVRC
Pune, University of Puna, EMRC
Roorkee, University of Roorkee, EMRC
Sagar, Dr Harisingh Gour Vishwavidyalaya, AVRC
Srinagar, University of Kashmir, AVRC

## REFERENCE

"Learning from UGC's Classrooms", in *The Economic Times*, 13 October 1993.

# 7. Calcutta Image, Mirage of Development

In the view of the poor, development as an international project and quite often even as a local project is a mirage. Development has never been promoted primarily for the benefit of those who need it most. After four decades of development policies and politics, there are more poor, more sick, more illiterate, more jobless, more shelterless than ever before. Cees Hamelink quotes the following figures: out of 5.6 billion persons more than one billion try to survive with less than US $370 per annum; one billion are illiterate; 500 million children do not go to school; and 30 per cent of the 2.8 billion workers are jobless.

But some of the rich nations too are disillusioned, as a large number of their people painfully experience a process of impoverishment. That should help these nations to understand that underdevelopment is not a natural stage which a community has to go through before development is achieved. Underdevelopment is a condition in which a society, in its totality, sinks like in quick-sands. The impoverishment which thousands of people are now experiencing in rich countries is development in reverse, underdevelopment.

Under the spell of a developmentalist ideology, we have committed ourselves to processes that we thought were essentially benevolent: progress, development and fulfilment of human potential. Now we begin to realise that, in fact, these forces were not at all in our service, but were functioning according to their own laws. These laws had nothing to do with our welfare. At one time, these forces did benefit some of us, like good weather at times does. But weather, good or bad, is not in the service of people: it serves no one, and it evolves according to its own laws. Similarly, development has its own laws, and these laws have finally been brought under the laws of the market.

The doctrine of the "free flow" that has now triumphed worldwide has consecrated *Homo Economicus*. On the altar of the market *Homo Economicus* has sacrificed the welfare of the planet. But the religious metaphor here is not appropriate. *Homo Economicus* is not a priest, but an entertainer. Whatever he does is a show. Example, the Gulf War. Sad to say, the Gulf War was more a matter of entertainment than a matter of concern. Have we—at least some among millions of people—not watched reports on the war as we watched football matches? But "patriots" and "scuds" were no footballs! When *Homo Economicus* blows up the planet, you won't miss the event, it will be on TV.

Since its foundation three hundred years ago, Calcutta has elicited several strong images in the minds of foreigners. "The City of Palaces", the "Pearl of the British Empire" or the "Black Hole". In the 1930s, anthropologist Claude Lévi-Strauss visited Calcutta. For him Calcutta was part of the *TRISTES TROPIQUES*, the pathetic tropics, and presented the sad image of what might become of the West.

After Lévi-Strauss came Dominique Lapierre, also from France. He wrote, not of his fear, but of his fascination for this city. For Lapierre Calcutta was not a fragment of some "tristes tropiques", but a city of joy, a block on which the development monument could be created.

The importance of that excellent novel—I do not speak here of the film which betrays the novel in several respects and which I criticise severely later in this book—resides in its vivid portrayal of a development agent working in a slum. Lapierre has illustrated the charity component of the developmentalist ideology. Everything is there: religious inspiration, absence of the political aspect, except for the implied justification of the politics of intervention in other people's affairs, the incapacity of the underdeveloped people to pull themselves out of their situation, the source of underdevelopment located in the "bad" local (of course!) people, the heroism and the beauty of the poor underdeveloped, even the depiction of underdevelopment as a milieu favourable to the eclosion of beautiful human virtues, like joy, for instance.

What had happened in the fifty years that elapsed between the visit of Lévi-Strauss and that of Lapierre? The two famous Frenchmen had different perceptions of Calcutta. The difference cannot be explained simply by the two writers' respective idiosyncrasies. The developmentalist ideology has caused Lapierre to see Calcutta the way he did.

In the early 1960s a Ford Foundation expert produced a document in which for the first time, perhaps, the mirage of development was made to scintillate over the image of Calcutta. True to the developmentalist ideology, development was seen in that document as a process to be handled by experts. Development could be planned and controlled like any other process amenable to scientific manipulation. In that view, humans have little place, except in terms of their number, their location, the epidemics they spread, the work they put in, the tremendous(!) threat they pose to the environment by cutting twigs from trees.

However, this blatant anti-human orientation of the developmentalist ideology was screened to an extent by charitable projects seeking to alleviate the distress of the underdeveloped. The powerful icon of Mother Teresa symbolises unconditional charity. The rise of Mother's icon in the Western psyche started precisely in the early sixties when the developmentalist ideology took hold of the political and administrative apparatus. In fact, as early as 1960 Mother featured in an article carried by the *Reader's Digest*. There are countless people in Calcutta who selflessly serve the poor the way Mother Teresa does. But Mother, quite apart from her personal charisma, has more appeal than they have in the Western media because development is essentially a project of the Christian West.

I hope I shall not be misunderstood; I do not wish to discourage those who devote themselves magnificently in the service of the poor. On the contrary, I wish to encourage them to continue and even to intensify their efforts. But I would also like to help them to see that we are all implicated in the condition of the poor and that some day we shall have to usher in a more just economic system whatever the cost. And it is important to know that it will cost us something whether one is rich or poor.

To usher in a more just economic system cannot be the work of one person only. Hope makes it possible to at least think of doing so. In the meantime the same hope inspires us and strengthens us to continue to help all those who suffer from various forms of poverty. For, that help really helps them. The late Cardinal Paul-Emile Léger (1904-91, former Archbishop of Montreal) funded some social projects in Pilkhana, the area of Calcutta nicknamed "The City of Joy" by Dominique Lapierre. The Cardinal visited the Pilkhana slum twice. He once asked, thinking of his financial contribution to the slum: "that is a mere drop of water in the ocean. Does that really help?" Came the reply from a social worker: "to get medicine when you have tuberculosis, that helps; to be given a meal when you are hungry, that helps; to get a blanket when you are cold, that helps. Some people look down on our work, saying that we do not solve the problems of these people. We care for people. It belongs to the government to solve problems." But the task is gigantic and the local government does not have all the means it requires. For, the roots of the problems are global; locally the poor get the bitter fruits. So, help helps.

In the 1970s the then President of the World Bank went on to say: "invest in the poor". The development of the poor was and remains absolutely essential to market-based imperialism. At the same time charity gives an opportunity to some Westerners to show that they "care", while it reassures others by the thought that whatever can be done is being done and nothing need be changed in the West.

Lapierre's book, *The City of Joy*, demonstrates, as it were, the validity of the development project. If it works in a Calcutta slum, then it must be right. The developmentalist ideology has it that the poor are nice people who deserve every possible help. Of course, it says, they are too many and they do all sorts of wrong things. But with some financial aid and a good amount of charity, they can be contained, cleaned, made aseptic and educated. Overpopulation will thus be averted and so will epidemics. Above all, the eye-sore will be prettified.

Yet, this optimism is not warranted. The economic reforms initiated from 1993 onward suggest that for the poor "Calcutta is for ever", as hoardings proclaimed during the city's tercentenary. Urban experts have released a report on the 100 largest cities of the world from the point of view of the habitat they constitute. Calcutta ranked among the four least liveable cities of the world. In spite of spectacular improvements (metro, bridge, flyovers, etc.) Calcutta continues to be underdeveloped.

The most apt image of Calcutta is perhaps that of a *trimurti*, an image with three faces. The face of cinéaste Satyajit Ray, the face of Mother Teresa, the face of the rickshaw puller in Dominique Lapierre's *The City of Joy*. Each face representing respectively the creativity of the intelligentsia, unconditional charity, and the heroism of an ordinary Calcuttan. That is my preferred image: it evokes human resources, compassion and hope.

## REFERENCES

Bedford, David and Pobishushchy, Sidney, "Towards a People's Economy: The Co-op Atlantic Experience" in *Interculture*, Vol. xxvi, No. 3, Summer 1993, issue 120.

Beland, Claude *et al.*, "Sortons le Québec de l'appauvrissement", Montreal, 9 March 1994.

Lapierre, Dominique, *The City of Joy*, London: Arrow Books, 1986 (Original French 1985).

Racine, Jean, ed., *Calcutta 1981: The City: Its Crisis and the Debate on Urban Planning and Development*, New Delhi: Concept Publishing Company, 1990 (Original French 1986).

Roberge, Gaston, "Images of Calcutta: From Black Hole to Black Box", in *Calcutta 1981*, Jean Racine, ed.

———, "Images of Calcutta: Mirages of Development", in *India International Centre Quarterly*, New Delhi, Spring-Summer 1993, pp. 225-42.

———, "Roland Joffe's *City of Joy*: *Fiction of a Wounded Psyche*", in *The Economic Times*, 17 November 1992, reproduced as chapter 33, pp. 99 and ff.

———, *The Ways of Film Studies, Film Theory and the Interpretation of Films*, New Delhi: Ajanta Books International, 1992 (Chapter 8: "Indian Icons", on Dominique Lapierre's *City of Joy*).

Zaoual, Hassan, "The Economy and the Symbolic Sites in Africa" in *Interculture*, Vol. xxvii, No. 1, Winter 1994, Issue 122. Zaoual speaks of a "culture of development", and of development as "an outgrowth of western culture". He says: "The utilitarian and productivist paradigm of development resembles a telescope where the West sees only itself, when it thinks it sees the Third World" (p. 23). The readiness with which we in India use the "telescope" shows how deeply the culture of development has colonised us.

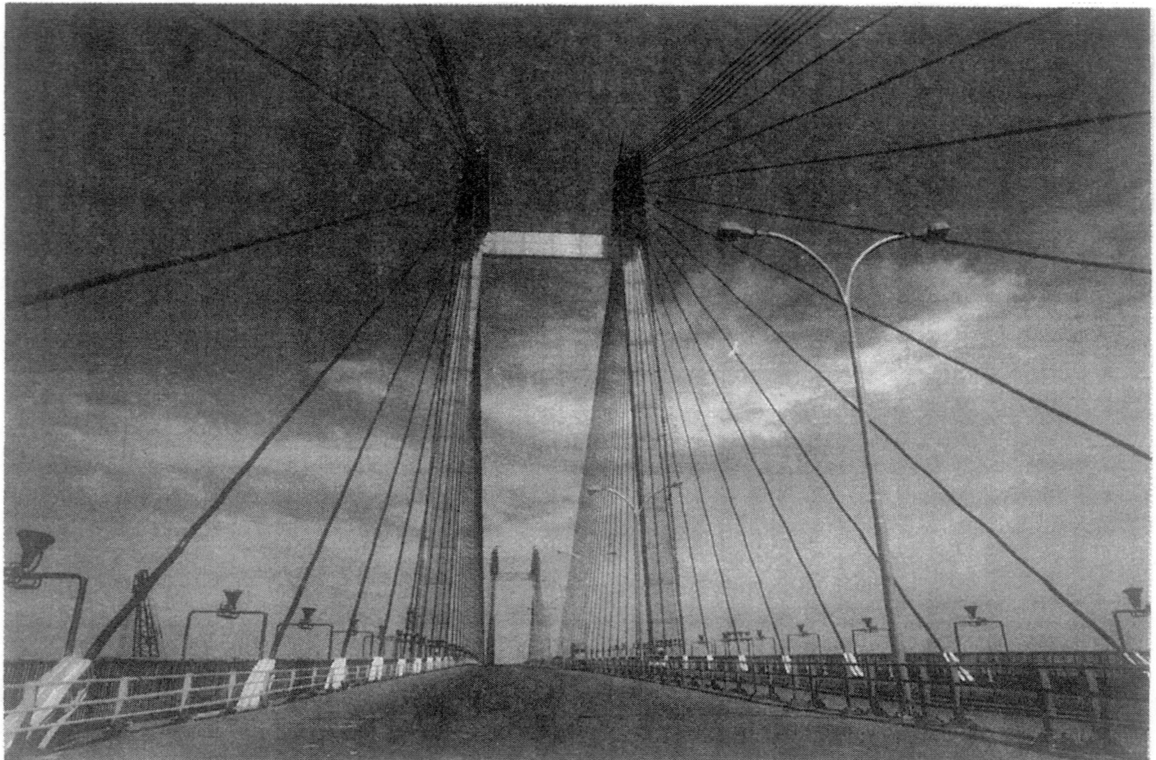

7. The economic reforms initiated recently suggest that for the poor *Calcutta is for ever*, to quote the slogan of the city on the occasion of its tercentenary.
Shilbhadra Datta

# 8. Not on Bread Alone, But on All Manners of Pictures

Early in 1979, the International Year of the Child, an exhibition of photographs was arranged in a slum of Calcutta. The photographs featured children of that very slum. For the first time in their lives these children saw pictures of themselves. And they liked what they saw. They brought their parents to see the exhibits. The parents too liked what they saw. It was a celebration. A mother stood by the side of her child's photo and proclaimed with great pride, "this is my boy, he is five year old, and he works, and he earns fifty paisas a day".

Yet, some local social workers commented, "photos are all very good. But what these people need is food, clothes, houses, medicines ...". To which they were told: "true, slum dwellers need all these things. And you social workers provide some of them. Yet, from their meagre earnings slum dwellers buy cinema tickets, they crowd the nearby cinema hall. They want pictures and they go to pictures."

For, man does not live on bread alone but on all manners of pictures.

Pictures may be graphic, as in the case of paintings, photographs, film and television, or literary, as in novels, for instance. Pictures are our main means of communication, and we, humans, could not do without them. That is why, the new manner in which pictures are generated today is a matter of concern and a cause of wonder. Computers and other advanced technologies make it possible to create pictures in ways never thought of before. Moreover, the relationship that these pictures bear with reality is also totally new. In fact, some pictures are not meant to refer to anything whatsoever outside themselves: they constitute a reality of its own. A "virtual" reality, but a reality none the less.

Amidst these new pictures, movies may seem something of the past, obsolete, anachronistic. But that is not the case. Today movies are not what they were yesteryear, and tomorrow they will be different. They endure. And movies too create virtual worlds. For instance, when you watch Satyajit Ray's *Charulata*, what do you watch? Surely not film actress Madhobi Mukherjee. You watch the unfolding of Charulata's world, a world that is imaginary, a world that is virtual. That world does not exist unless you make it exist in your mind. The film provides the basis for your mind to work on, but the virtual world of Charulata exists for you and thanks to you.

However, "Virtual Reality" (VR) or "cyberspace", to use the name coined by science fiction writer William Gibson in 1984, goes much further than cinema. VR technology gives you a sense of being in a space, a cyberspace, which an ordinary movie cannot provide. The movie offers a two-dimensional picture, and although the camera gives you views from different angles, you are always in a fixed position in front of the flat screen.

With the help of a helmet fitted with big goggles, a special glove with electronic wiring, and perhaps a treadmill for you to move your feet on, VR technology watches the reactions of your eyes, hands and feet, and it responds accordingly. For example, suppose your monitor presents a picture of a large hall, you want to see what's there, on the right hand side, and you turn your eyes in that direction. Then your monitor changes the view and shows you what you'd see if you were inside the hall and looked towards your right hand side. So, with VR technology, not only can you imagine space as you do while watching a movie, but you get a feel of being inside that space. In addition to vision various other sense organs of the body are fed by the computer to simulate a virtual environment. The next step is for you to yourself create a virtual world and inhabit it.

These new image-making technologies and their interaction with computers were developed in the ambit of the defense industry, especially in the USA. But the virtual worlds that we come to know of today were first imagined and even experimented with by people belonging to film and entertainment. Unfortunately, money was not made available to these people. The defense industry patronized more down-to-earth scientists. It is they who realised the dreams of earlier film-makers, and, irony of history, they did it partly with the money brought in by video games.

1995 marks cinema's one hundredth year. But in the light of VR it can be said that cinema is still in its infancy. Nonetheless, practitioners of the art and its specialised consumers, namely, the critics and the film scholars, have constituted a solid body of scholarly reflection. That scholarship should be a great help in our effort at understanding the new technologies of image-making and the virtual worlds they make possible. For, these virtual worlds are, in fact, developments of the cinema.

Film studies constitute a necessary basis for probing cyberspace because of their interdisciplinary approach involving psychoanalysis, women's studies, linguistics and semiology, and international communication. But more importantly still, film studies cultivate the very attitude which is required to study virtual worlds: a will to take images seriously, a certain confidence that they are relevant, an unshakable certainty that they have meaning.

That is why film studies are more necessary than ever. Film studies deal with the various aspects of films, in themselves and in their relation with both those who make them and those who consume them. Unfortunately, this academic discipline has not yet developed in India in relation with India's particular cultures, arts, entertainments, religions and social groups. Unless we catch up with that academic field we shall be at a great disadvantage in front of virtual reality as it will soon be offered to our masses.

By and large, we are unable to deal rationally with the most popular films, like *Beder Meye Josna* (Bangladesh 1990, remade in West Bengal and analysed in chapter 32) or *Roja*. Millions of people saw these films, many of them several times. Few have understood that the popularity of these films is due to the fact that the films have a direct link to contemporary socio-political events. We are told by psychoanalysts that an individual's dream always deal with the immediate reality of the dreamer. As collective dreams, films always deal with the immediate reality of the public that see those films. These films may lack realism in the way they deal with their subjects, but the subjects themselves always are utterly realist. For the subjects, even if they are disguised, as it were, by the films, are lifted from the life of the audience. When we fail to acknowledge that fact what can our response be to "virtual reality"?

That "virtual reality" will rarely be of our making, still more rarely of our liking. For, more and more foreign films are available to Indian viewers. The doctrine of "free flow" that has now triumphed worldwide has always meant a one-way flow. And by adopting the free market economy we have lost control over the alien cultural products available in our country. The least we can do is to regain intellectual control over the phenomenon. And one way to do this is to foster film studies throughout the country.

## REFERENCES

Rheingold, Howard, *Virtual Reality*, Martin Secker & Warburg Limited, 1991, Mandarin Paperbacks, 1992.

Schiller, Herbert I. *et al.*, *The Ideology of International Communications*, Institute of Media Analysis, Inc., N.Y., Monograph Series, No. 4, 1992.

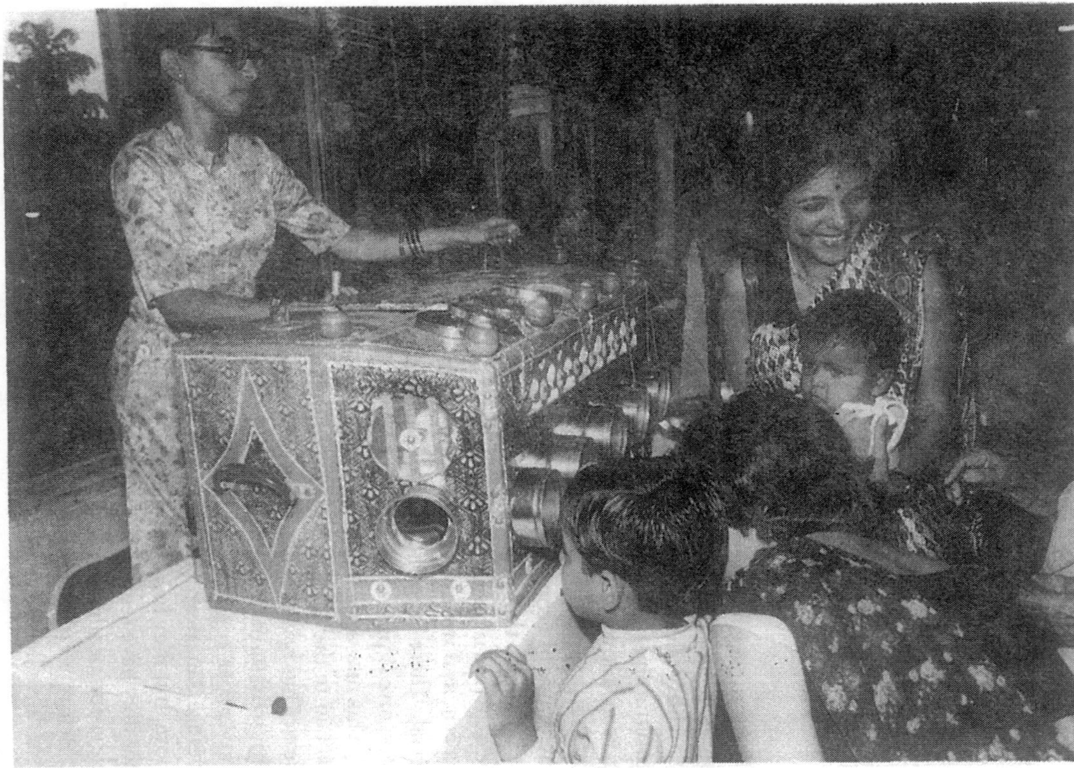

8. For man does not live on bread alone . . . but on all manners of pictures.
Salim Paul

# 9. Fourteen Years of Rigorous TV Watching for Every Citizen

The sentence has been passed: every person likely to live up to sixty-five years is condemned to spend at least fourteen years of his waking life watching television. In case one should escape, he would be cut off from entertainment, from the knowledge of what every knowledgeable person knows (like the score of the latest football match), from the threats and promises of advertising, from the comedy of politics, from the drama of economics, from the sweet terror generated by witnessing at a distance the calamities occurring to others, and above all he would be deprived of moments of emptiness when, possessed by the television screen, as if under hypnosis, one can forget everything for the time of a serial. There is no choice. Indeed, the sentence is a double-bind. Either way, one is punished.

This may appear to refer to a distant, imaginary land. In fact, the data pertain to the USA. It is reported that the average American television viewer has by the age of 65 spent 3000 entire days watching television. This works out to nine full years or 14 waking years watching television. Newspaper reports also have it that by the end of high school, the average American boys and girls have spent 11,000 hours in the classroom, but they have watched 15,000 hours of television, which means that they have seen 350,000 commercials and witnessed 18,000 violent television deaths.

Before we dismiss these facts as irrelevant to our Indian situation we'd do well to have a look at the "Preliminary Report on the Impact of TV on Secondary School Children" prepared in 1993-4 by the State Council of Educational Research & Training, Govt. of West Bengal. The Council surveyed nearly 775 students from 27 schools in cities, industrial areas and villages. It appears that 84 per cent of the high school students surveyed watch TV everyday especially in the evenings for about 3 to 4 hours. But nearly 25 per cent of the students spend more than 5 hours daily watching television. We'll catch up with America very soon. And the prospect of spending nearly 20 per cent of our waking lives in front of a TV set is already open to us here in India.

But are we really condemned to watch TV? Can we not remain free in front of the TV set? Suppose one could plan one's life from the very first year of existence, would one want to invest as much as 20 per cent of one's life in TV watching? Would not one plan for oneself a more rewarding time table?

There are people—few, in fact—who snub television and pride themselves with the fact that "there is no TV in our home". Frankly, such stoicism is not called for. Reasonable use of TV may be wiser than proud rejection. Although television watching is somewhat addictive, it just cannot be equated to a hard drug calling for a firm "no".

And is not the description of TV watching proposed above a bit of a "mala fide" caricature? Or, since there are people who use television that way, is it not an unwarranted generalisation? Are we condemned to such a desperate position in front of the television monitor? Surely not. But there are difficulties.

The greatest difficulty arises, it seems, from the exiguity of our homes. When the television set is on, there may be no other place where to sit for anyone who would like not to watch TV. This is a serious problem for students. Some sacrifice and rational time management will have to be considered. That is, the family may perhaps have to sacrifice certain programmes in order to allow some quiet in the home for students to do their home tasks and studies. On the other hand, students may have to manage their time more thoughtfully in order to accommodate both their tasks as students and watching of some TV programmes.

Ideally, one could think of community study rooms where a few students could do their work without being disturbed or tempted by television.

One thing is sure, some television-free spaces have to be created or, if it is not already too late, preserved. I am speaking primarily of physical space. But the discipline required to create or preserve physical spaces free from television, helps one develop the discipline required to use television critically and freely.

It would be stupid not to receive from television whatever knowledge it can offer. It would be childish to refuse to be aware of what is happening in the world, although it can be argued that newspapers provide better information than television. One is or can be more detached in front of a newspaper, one may also have access to more than a paper and thus compare the ways a particular news item is presented.

In general, a certain sense of humour might help. One should not take television too seriously. There is something playful in much of television. As for the rest, perhaps we can get a hint from other studies of television watching made among American children. It was found that at a very early age all children watch TV eagerly and all seem to learn something or other from it. But slowly some of the children shift to what they consider more rewarding activities, like playing games, drawing or reading. They may well be right those people who think that the children who limit their TV watching to certain types of programmes are cleverer and happier than those who cannot detach themselves from the TV screen. It is well worth pondering over that.

Meanwhile it is urgent to realise that television is part of our environment. It is up to each one to relate meaningfully to that environment. If the TV set could address the viewer, it might well ask, "why do you call me 'idiot box', when you readily stare at me for hours every day? Am I not your antenna on the world? Am I not a faithful companion in your loneliness? Am I not your uptodate encyclopaedia? Am I not your court jester? Am I not your personal advisor? You,...! wise among the wise!"

## REFERENCES

*Educommunication-News*, Quarterly Bulletin, Bruxelles, June 1994, No. 27, p. 9.

Ray, Dipak and Surja Sankar Ray, "Preliminary Report on the Impact of TV on Secondary School Children". The State Council of Educational Research & Training, Govt. of West Bengal, January 1994.

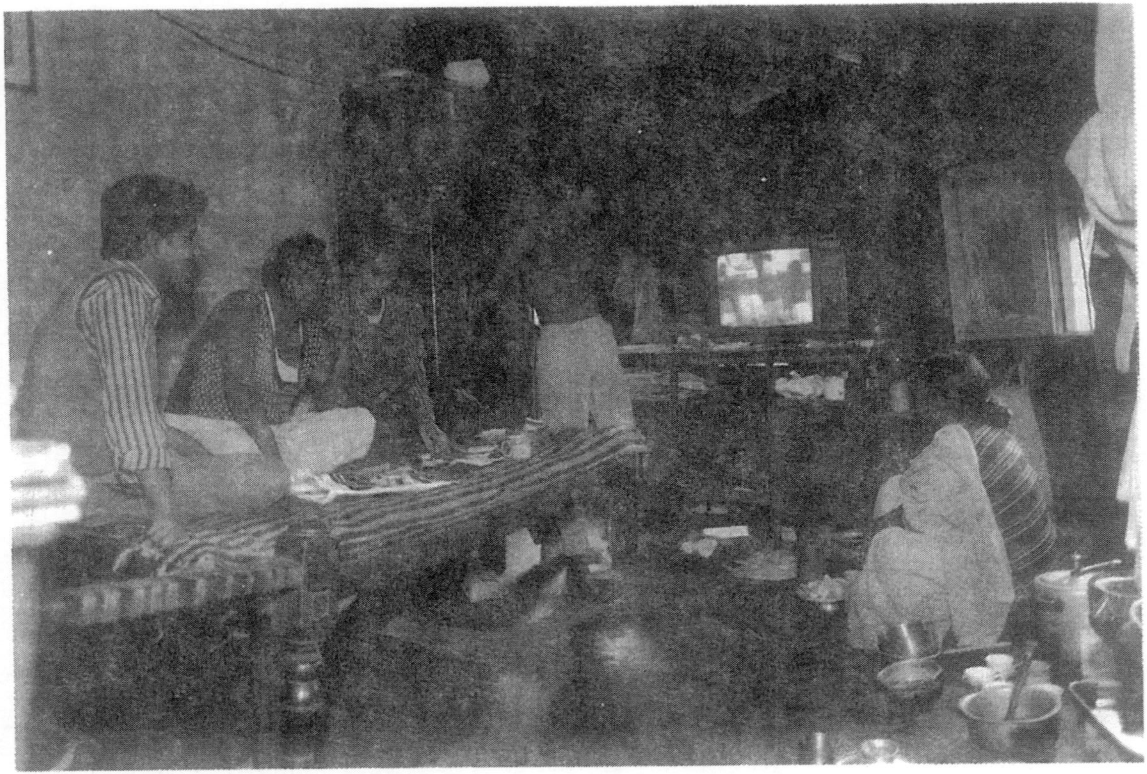

9. The prospect of spending nearly 20 per cent of our waking lives in front of a TV set is already open to us here in India.
Shilbhadra Datta

# 10. Rape! Rape! Rape!

In the beginning of the 1990s there were so many scenes of rapes in Indian films that the Central Board of Certification felt it had to issue special instructions to its members. Rape scenes were to be so cut as to leave only the beginning, where the intention of raping is manifest, and the end, where the consequences of the rape are shown, for instance, the rapist being beaten up or, more often, the woman bemoaning her fate.

Rape was thus considered as a purely sexual behaviour demeaning the victim, usually a woman. The old obsession of the censorship boards with sex, and the new pretense of a concern for the dignity of women dictated the policy. But such a policy is only as good as censorship, and censorship is no good.

Rape is not just a sexual behaviour. And hence it does not affect the nature of a rape scene if you shorten it by removing the manoeuvres, presumably more sexy, leading to the sex act. On the other hand, the dignity of women is not protected by simply getting the rape done faster. The fact remains, a person is raped.

The increase in the number of rape scenes in films is paralleled by an increase in the reports of rapes in newspapers. Rape cases are perhaps not more frequent today than they were previously, but there certainly is more talk about them, due, in good part, to the feminist movement. Unfortunately, censorship of whatever name, like, for instance, "certification", is unable to deal with social problems. And rape is indeed a social issue.

The fact is, rape sells well: as a news item and as a spectacle. A producer who had stuffed as many as five rape scenes in one film objected to the shortening of these scenes demanded by the board of certification. He told the members of the board, "What do you think I make films for? It's to make money. ... If you shorten all these scenes, how am I to make money?"

The feminists may have brought rape in the limelight, but they have not contributed to a full understanding of it. That is because of their specific, limited, point of view. For, rape does not concern women only. Men do rape other men too. Moreover, rapes are often perpetrated not by one but by a group of men. These two facts should help in realising that there is in rape something more than the sexual urge.

Rape is a manner of communication among men, or of a man in monologue within himself. The body, most of the time female, is the medium. And what is the message? The message has to do with revenge, fear, hatred, and contempt for women, fuelled by insecurity about one's "masculinity" and capacity to "perform" as a man.

It is said that during the nine-month liberation war of Bangladesh in 1971, two to four lakhs women were raped by the enemy. The lack of precision in the figures is symptomatic of the difficulty women have to talk about rape. What the figures, even though imprecise, mean is that a large number of women were raped. Surely, the soldiers did not perpetrate these crimes only because of a sudden sexual urge. And the rapes of women in Bangladesh are paralleled by rapes in Vietnam and in so many other countries at war.

Furthermore, rapes are only one aspect of a larger problem, namely, the victimisation of women. The beating of women at home is one of the best guarded domestic secrets. In such incidents both male and female are caught in double binds that are themselves pathological and generate more pathology: the husband wants to ensure that "his" woman will respect him as her master but he looses her respect by beating her; the woman fears that if she speaks out she will be immediately victimised, and if she does not speak out she will continue to be victimised.

In patriarchal societies the attitude that leads to rape and to the victimisation of women is deeply rooted. Among the Hebrews, the spiritual ancestors of the white colonial powers, when the number of people was computed women were not considered, except along with the cattle. Since the subjection of women is not a natural state of affairs, it is necessary for any society where women are thus subjected to ensure that women conform to their imposed status.

A long process of socialisation moulds the personality of children: the girl child is sure to develop "feminine" qualities, and the boy child is trained to "behave like a man". Meanwhile the myth of the sensitive, intuitive, woman and the logical, practical, man is perpetuated by the mass media. A popular brand of suitcases, for instance, has recently articulated its advertising campaign on gender distinction and roles. In the process, the campaign is likely to have contributed to "sell" the stereotyped images, especially of the woman as either a future mother, a mother or one who was a mother.

It is feared that the present fare of television programmes worldwide fosters male chauvinism and trains viewers to accept violence as a way of life. At the same time the view that women enjoy being raped and being dealt with roughly is strengthened among men. Research reports on television and behaviour, it is true, are based mostly on American television and viewership. But these reports may be dismissed as one more foreign concern only by one who believes that American television is far from the Indian home. According to some of these reports, the effects of televised violence may be even deeper and more extensive than they are thought to be. For, while some viewers may be encouraged to violent behaviour, others, perhaps the majority, may learn to identify with victims. This latter effect may be very damaging but it remains practically undetected.

As can be seen, the issue of rape is very complex, not just a matter arousing indignation. It is a form of male communication and it is fantasied by the most pervasive communication media, the press, film and television.

# 11. AIDS Literacy

AIDS is with us. We have to live with it. And to live with it decently, we have to talk about it. But to understand what is said about AIDS or to talk about AIDS, you need to master a jargon that amounts to a specialised literacy. Words like AIDS or Aids, to start with, and then HIV, HIV 1, HIV 2, sero-positive, window period, antibody positive, and the like constitute "Aidspeak". This is a complex and highly emotional language, dealing all at once with love, sex, life and death. Indeed, the AIDS epidemic has triggered a language epidemic.

As a result, there may be some confusion in the mind of the AIDS "illiterate" as to who has what. In fact, a person said to have AIDS, has first acquired a virus, the famous HIV or Human Immuno-Deficiency Virus. The virus has weakened the organism in a period of time which can be as long as ten years. Then the weakened organism fell prey to any infection that happened to be around. In India, for instance, people with HIV often contract tuberculosis. Normally, tuberculosis is curable. But this is not so when a person is weakened by HIV. The condition of the person having a terminal infection, after being weakened by HIV, is labelled AIDS, that is, "Acquired Immuno Deficiency Syndrome". And a syndrome is a group of signs or symptoms. So, from the time one acquires the virus called HIV until the time one develops a terminal infection one passes through various stages. At first one has HIV only. But in time one develops "full blown AIDS". Naturally, in day to day conversation, people cannot always be that accurate. AIDS is often used when HIV would be more correct as, for instance, in the phrase "the AIDS virus".

Once "Aidspeak" is mastered, one realizes that, since all communication establishes or strengthens a power structure, communication about AIDS too is enmeshed in power networks. Thus, what appeared to be only a disease and primarily a biological phenomenon, comes to be seen for what it is, namely, a messy battlefield where various formations confront each other: medical, cultural, political, economic, psychological, spiritual and ideological.

In the biological sphere the AIDS epidemic was powered by a virus. But in the social sphere the power came from the two main establishments that claim control over our lives: the medical and the religious. The medical establishment affirmed its sole right to name the virus (and thus to be entrusted with gigantic sums of money to conduct "research"—this idol of our scientific cultures). Two heads of state met and solemnly agreed on a name for the virus. That was an international event. On the other hand, the religious establishment affirmed its sole right to determine which behaviour is "natural" and "according to God's will". The medical establishment grossed immense profits. A pharmaceutical firm, it is said, made one million dollars profit in only one year through manufacturing an anti-AIDS medicine which only a few privileged rich could afford to buy. As for the religious establishment, it suffered a heavy loss of credibility and thus of real power.

But these establishments did not go unchallenged: groups that were isolated or even victimised for having contracted the virus answered back: firstly the people having same sex behaviour and then the women activists.

However, those who most often are spoken about when official discourses refer to the "people at risk", or the "AIDS victims" are not "authorised" to speak for themselves. So, they had first to activate their rightful power to speak. They demanded that persons having the virus be not called "victims". Especially objectionable was the phrase "innocent victims" when referring to persons who acquired the virus by blood transfusion. For, the phrase implies that people who have contracted the virus through other means, like sexual behaviour, for instance, were not innocent. Activists demanded also that persons with the virus be not called "patients". Because persons having the virus do not necessarily develop symptoms of sickness, at least for some time. And these people need not be hospitalised, still less quarantined. Even persons having developed symptoms called AIDS need not be segregated though some cases may have to be hospitalised. So, the phrase "people with AIDS" (PWA) was coined by activists. But since having AIDS implies death after some time, the phrase "people living with AIDS" was suggested as more hopeful and positive.

But in addition to creating new phrases expressive of their specific concerns, activists had to resort to parallel methods of communication because they did not have access to the mass media. One such alternative or parallel method of communication was the "AIDS Memorial Quilt". Activists realised that as long as people have not been touched personally by the affliction or even the death of someone close to them, they wish AIDS away. They think that AIDS involves only other people. They think of AIDS as a problem others have. In order to personalise the problem and bring it closer to everyone, that is, in order to shift attention from virus (the problem) to persons (who have problems), the activists felt that those who had died of AIDS complications should be mourned and their names should be uttered. Quilting would be the medium. A quilt is a blanket made of pieces of cloth stitched together. Quilting or making quilts used to be a folk craft in the USA. Quilts often formed interesting patterns and displayed a high degree of creativity. For the AIDS Memorial Quilt, any one person could prepare a piece of cloth, two by three feet in size, on which the name of a person having died of AIDS was written. These pieces of cloth were stitched together to form an immense quilt.

The quilt was displayed in Washington, D.C. in October 1989. It covered the 14 acres of the Ellipse and was made of nearly eleven thousand panels. It constituted a public artwork and a form of mourning that proved religious funerals or literary elegies to be inadequate in the case of those having died of AIDS. As a communication medium quilting paralleled the dominant communication media and revived an old folkloric tradition.

Literacy in general is not just a matter of words. A literate person is conversant with books and literature. Similarly, AIDS literacy is not just a matter of jargon. An AIDS literate person is conversant with the discourse, the rhetorics and the symbols through which power is exercised in the creation and management of the AIDS phenomenon.

In October 1994 the number of persons having HIV in India was estimated to be 15,562, and the number of full blown AIDS cases 803. However alarming these figures are, they do not seem to warrant the large sums of money that are spent on pharmaceutical research and on AIDS education. It is difficult to anticipate the progress of the pandemic. At the time of writing, 4 million children die each year from diseases related to unsafe drinking water and inadequate sanitation (*Time International*, 7 November 1994, pp. 40-1). This is by far more than can be foreseen to die of AIDS in the future. On the other hand, the discourse on AIDS generates intractable paradoxes. In particular, the issue of testing has divided the world into those who have HIV, and those who do not have it. Since without a test one cannot know whether one has HIV or does not have it, one does not know for sure who one is until one has been told by a test. Meanwhile what is one to do? In order to be safe one should "abstain" totally. Thus, the best way not to die is not to live!

The 31 October 1994 issue of *Time* (International edition) carried a one page advertisement (for what else call the page?) sponsored by the New Delhi office of UNDP. I do not doubt the good intention of those who prepared the text, but I am hurt by the non- or in-human language of the message. It says, "Thanks to AIDS, many companies will soon be depositing their assets here." And there is an image of tomb stones in a cemetery. Clever. But the sole consideration is that, "if your worker leaves the company as a result (of acquiring HIV), it will cost you money to find a replacement". True. So "keep AIDS out of your business". Wise. And the text concludes, "you've probably spent a fortune training your employees. Doesn't it make sense to protect your investment by spending a little more on teaching them about AIDS? They are, after all, your most valuable assets." Outrageous! How can a prestigious organisation like UNDP demean industrialists, managers, entrepreneurs by assuming that the only language they can understand is that of cold business? Does it not make sense to any person in business to protect those serving the business because they are fellow humans? Of course, that one publicity page does not represent all the activities, still less all the concerns, of the agency. My criticism, therefore, bears only on the page.

## REFERENCES

Dean, Tim, "The Psychoanalysis of AIDS", in October, Winter 1993, pp. 83-116.

Erni, John, "Articulating the Impossible: Popular Media and the Cultural Politics of 'Curing AIDS'", in *Communication*, 1992, Vol. 13, pp. 39-56.

Hahon, Alvis, "Talking about AIDS", in *Materialities of Communication* (Original German 1988), edited by Hans Ulrich Gumbrecht and K. Ludwig Pfeiffer, California: Stanford University Press, 1994, pp. 344-54.

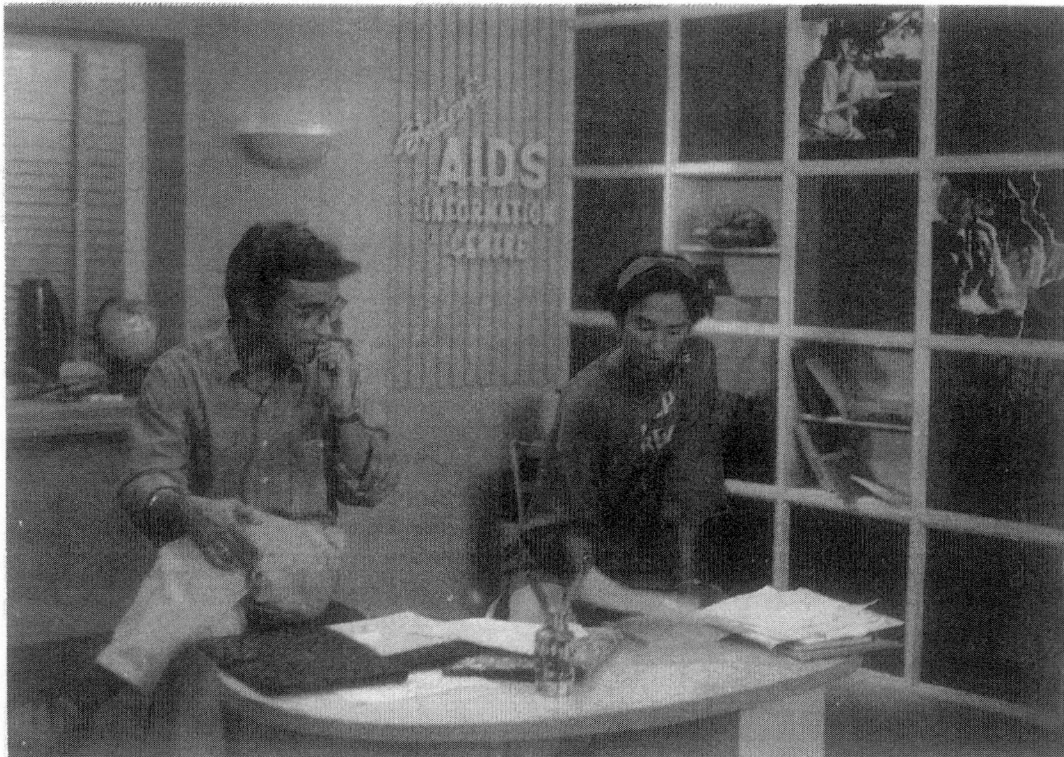


10. AIDS is with us. We must live with it. And in order that we may live with it reasonably, it is necessary to speak about it. This picture is a production still of a television spot produced by Chitrabani and telecast by the UGC's *Countrywide Classroom*.
Shilbhadra Datta

# 12. The Man/Woman Fault

We, men, see women, a woman or "the" woman from a man's point of view (What other point of view can a man have?). Thus, women are our mothers, our sisters, our wives, our daughters, our friends, our lovers and, at times, forgive me for mentioning it, our mistresses, whose masters we think we are.

But surely, a woman is a human before and apart from being any of the above. She exists without these possessive, man-centred, relationships. She cannot be defined solely in terms of what she is to man. Yet, how to speak of her? Words—at least in English—fail us: for, a *woman* is a hu*man*, one of *man*kind. Man. Man. Man. Irremediably?

Man does not know woman, and woman does not know man. The divide '/' cannot be crossed over. But is there a man honest enough to say he does not know anything about woman?

Knowing nothing about woman, men could not write "about" woman, so, for centuries they wrote woman. They defined and confined, they described and prescribed, they eulogised and condemned, they married and divorced. They psychoanalysed both men and women to help them adjust to their respective vocations which, if need be, could be shown to be divine. All the while, men created an imperfect man, "the second sex", the verso of man who by nature will for ever stand versus man. What has been conceived opposite cannot be reconciled.

But how does one become a man, how does one become a woman? Not by birth. By training. Both man and woman are manufactured by civilisation. It is believed that by the age of four a child has become a small man or a small woman. The boy knows that, a boy, he is or should be logical, active, strong. The girl should be intuitive, passive, weak. These qualities probably have nothing to do with the biological constitution of either the boy or the girl. But a boy soon behaves like a boy, and a well brought up girl, like a girl. Up to very recently there were jobs that befitted girls, others boys, in keeping with the attributes of both. Thus, the divide was created. Could not love cut across?

To be sure we, men, love women above all. Romeo and Tristram and Majnu and every toreador on earth would lay their lives for Juliet, Isolde, Laila or Carmen. Then, why do men treat women so badly? Too often a girl-child is not fed properly, is not allowed to attend school. Too often she is used life long for domestic chores: her patient labour, conveniently, is free. A wife, too often she is abused, beaten up. She is teased, she is raped. Should she die—as all humans must—her husband becomes free, he may happily remarry. But, a widow, too often her hair is cut, too often she is secluded in mourning for months, she is even burnt. For we, gentlemen, burn widows, witches and heretics. Is a woman, then, just a man of woe, a woman?

We, gentle men, fear fair women. Yet, we fix our gaze on women, we desire them. Fear compounded with desire conjure up the sublime, the mystique. And we celebrate woman in poem after poem. We project her to the far side of our anxious imaginations. We make of her "Our Lady" to embody the utterly other, the unfathomable mystery. We think of her as the virgin-mother of all men and women on earth. Or in time of nationalism, when every one feels like a motherless child, we see her as the mother "par excellence", Mother India, providing both existence and identity.

Man has created this remote, indeed impossible, ideal: woman sans sex. For, presumably, sex is sin. And the woman of man's dream, is at once sans sex and sans sin. What a contradiction! Man would not wish to possess a woman forced onto such a procrustean bed. But, in fact, man does not want to possess woman so much as he wants to desire her. And desire is only of the impossible.

But can woman be a sister to man—let alone a mother—unless she is a sinner? How confused things have become! Firstly, sex is no sin. Secondly, one need not be a sinner in order to be a human, though experience shows that most men and women are sinners. Thirdly, love, not sin, sustains fellowship. Moreover, those who sin least know sinners best. This is only apparently paradoxical. For, sin smoke-screens the self and the sinner looses sight of the self.

The man/woman divide is a fault of the type one finds on the surface of the earth. The earth does not fall apart because of a fault. But the parts on either sides of the fault are submitted to extreme pressure. The artificial fault created on the surface of the human group is maintained through a violent repression of the individuals brought up as women.

Shall man, then, ever know woman, and woman ever know man?

No. Because they have been so cultivated as to remain unknowable to each other. But Kamal most surely can know Kamala, and vice-versa. That is, a he-person can know a she-person. There lies the hope and the difficulty. To be a person. Only a person can know man or woman as person. A de-personalised "he" cannot see a woman as a person: he can only perceive her as an object or as one performing a function. The person in man must be restored. And in woman too. But how? A sister once cried: "who will save us? who will heal our wounded humanity?"

That cry had healing power.

In order to be able to make his or hers that cry a man or a woman has to first acknowledge the "fault", the flaw, the wound in our humanity. That is not a moralistic, guilt ridden concern, but a realisation borne out of the experience of suffering. Suffering of all sorts: pain, of course, physical or moral, but also the awareness of so much that is unfulfilled in us, partly due to our negligence, mostly for no fault of ours. That suffering is not passive, nor is it heroic or sublime. Johann Baptist Metz wrote:

> Suffering, which makes us cry out or finally fall wretchedly silent, knows no majesty. It is nothing great, nothing sublime; at root it is something entirely different from a powerful, solidaristic suffering with. It is not simply a sign of love, rather, it is much more a horrifying sign of no longer being able to love. It is that suffering which leads intó nothingness if it is not a suffering unto God. (Metz: p. 619)

By "suffering unto God" Metz means a suffering that questions God with vibrant expectations while knowing that God, indeed, speaks, but does not answer our questions.

The fault I have described above is created and maintained by verbal language: masculine and feminine. That language prevents communication between man and woman. At the same time, that language prevents the individual from fully defining himself or herself as a human being. Most obviously, the development of humankind demands that the fault be mended. But the point is not primarily to make woman equal to man. For man does not suffer less than woman from the fault. More profoundly the aim is to redefine the terms of the relation man-woman so as to allow among the two a free and liberating communication.

Unfortunately, the various feminist movements that militate for the liberation of the woman are often themselves marked with the human fault. For, it is the couple man-woman that has to be liberated; man no less than woman. If the woman is dominated, then the man dominates.

Moreover, what would a woman gain in being the equal of a "faulted" man. Both men and women are faulted. And no one can say, "Gender inequality is not *my* fault."

When Catholic women claim as a right access to the status of a priest, do they not give too much importance to the clergy and in the same claim do they not strengthen the clericalism that is rampant in the Church and of which they are the first victims? On the other hand, when international development agencies tell us that women hold the key to development, when the same agencies advocate and support various health and education programmes for women, do they seek economic development or development of the woman? Everything suggests that the main preoccupation is economic. Which means that, according to these developmentalist projects women will have to supplement the income of their family (since the wages paid to the men are insufficient) in addition to bear and educate children, care for their husbands and often enough for their parents as well. The development of the woman in these projects, consists in making the woman capable to fulfil two functions. Many thanks! That's good news, indeed. But for whom?

And you, my sisters, rejoice. I do not need to be an angel to tell you, Future generations will call you blessed for the omnipotents have looked upon you with kindness. Those among you who were considered unproductive will now be mothers twice over, mothers of children and mothers of development.

## REFERENCE

Metz, Johann Baptist, "Suffering Unto God", in *Critical Inquiry*, Summer 1994, Vol. 20, No. 1, pp. 611-22.

# 13. Maidan Virtual

Cinema is hardly one hundred years old, and we, viewers, have not yet mastered its language. We have not yet fully comprehended the worlds it opens up to us. These worlds are often the private inner spaces of film-makers, more often though, they are the collective inner spaces of entire societies. But, however vividly these spaces appear in front of us, they exclude us as spectators. Now we hear of worlds created by an array of audio and video hardware interfacing with computers and giving the user the impression that he enters the monitor's screen and moves in the computer world, that is, in cyberspace. When we can hardly find our way in cinema worlds, how shall we survive in cyberspace?

The worlds of cinema were thought to reflect "reality" and they generally came to us clothed in a certain naturalness, a verisimilitude that made them look somewhat like the reality we live in. But cyberspace knows no such constraints. It rarely looks like day-to-day reality and it need not reflect anything outside of itself. It is a reality of its own.

At the same time as we hear of virtual reality we witness with a sense of helplessness the process of globalisation in both the economic and communication fields. From our experience of watching television from outside, as it were, we have serious reasons to feel ill at ease at the prospect of getting inside the TV world. We wonder whether we shall have any freedom in the space created by computers.

Yet, the new communications technologies have already shown us, here in India, interesting possibilities which most of us would not have dreamt of even a few years ago. For instance, both the Indira Gandhi National Open University (IGNOU) and the UGC COUNTRYWIDE CLASSROOM have demonstrated nationwide the possibility of interactive television. Students watched educational programmes and by telephone addressed questions to experts. The student asking a question by telephone could not be seen, but he could be heard on the entire network and everyone watching the show could both see and hear the expert giving his answer.

That was a far cry from the creation of a virtual, totally computer generated, world, but it made it possible for students and telespectators to experiment with the medium of television. They realised that the spectators need not be as passive as they perhaps thought. Another interesting demonstration of a use of television is teleconferencing. This too has been done in India a number of times. Three or four persons located in as many different places can be seen on the television screen and can be heard talking to each other as if there was no distance between them, as if, indeed they occupied the same space.

Yet, perhaps the most heartening television event was that put up by a German television company in Hamburg, in 1993. The company created what might well be a real communication-utopia, a communicopia. They called their event *Piazza Virtuale*, that is, the "virtual town square", from the Italian word piazza or place.

*Piazza virtuale* was a "town square" of global dimension. Anyone having access to a phone and to a television set could join in on the virtual *piazza*. And people did join in. According to press reports, around 5,000 people phoned the first day. Next day, one lakh people phoned. In all, during the 100 days of the *piazza*, nearly 30,000 got on the air. These people could activate a mobile camera hovering from the ceiling of the television studio. The caller became the camera person. There were no anchor-persons, no journalists, no comperes. The user could either watch the technical crew inside the studio or speak, shout, harangue, dance, draw, sing: he or she was on the public square. Up to twenty people could get on the air at a time and discuss together (the neo-fascist riots in Rostock, Germany, which had just occurred at the time, are said to have been the topic of heated discussion).

The company that created *piazza virtuale* was formed as recently as in 1986. It does not telecast "commercials", but operates from grants and donations. The staff of the company have no contracts. They are there because they want to be there, and they get an honorarium commensurate to needs, not greed.

The *piazza virtuale* drew the attention of one of the main television networks in Japan who got the German company to create a virtual public place for the Japanese. The Japanese too joined in. That was in August 1993. There were so many phone calls that the telephone system jammed. Now the same German company has been approached to again create a *piazza virtuale*, this time from Atlanta, during the Olympic Games in 1996. The *piazza* would include anyone watching the games.

The *piazza* experiment re-introduces the human element in the hardware. In doing so, it re-introduces culture, in its diversity. The idea of the *piazza* arises from a consciousness that the man-machine relationship will be central in most cultures in the world brought about by globalisation. There is a fear that the relationship will prove the doom of humans. The *piazza virtuale* demonstrates that, far from dominating humans, the new communication technologies, when used creatively, can enhance human life and extend the reach of its cultures.

Each culture organises its space for public gathering and communication in a manner characteristic of that culture. One can think of the Athenian Agora where the Greeks first experimented with what they called somewhat mistakenly democracy. One can think of the Roman "forum". One can think of so many other famous and infamous "squares" throughout the world. In Calcutta, there is the Maidan, a place to relax, to meet people, to listen to songs, to sell products, to display animals, to put up "street plays" (presumably maidan plays), to discuss issues of cosmic relevance, to relish favourite snacks, and at times to join large political rallies.

The metaphors created to describe and name the possibilities offered by new media technologies are good indicators of culture. The Americans speak of electronic highways while the European used the image of a public square. We, people of the maidan, would feel more comfortable on a piazza than on a highway. And it is quite possible for us to think of a *Maidan Virtual*, open to all our people and even to people from abroad, but having the cultural characteristics of our Indian maidans.

For the time being, Internet has not yet spread over India. But several "nets" are already there. Film-maker Abel Gance once (1929) wrote with great enthusiasm about cinema: "The time of the image is upon us.... We, at least some of us, are riding on cloud horses, and when we battle it is with reality, trying to transform it into dream." We, in turn could well say, "the time of the 'net' is upon us". The metaphor of the net is fascinating; a nervous net around the globe making possible instantaneous communication. Will the Americans transform the net into an information highway? I hope they won't. For a highway always goes some definite places. A highway always is policed. On the Internet, on the contrary, you go where you will, even in uncharted territory.

## REFERENCES

Agel, Henri, *Esthétique du Cinéma*, Presses Universitaires de France, 1966.
Marshall, Jules, "The Medium is the Mission", in *Wired*, November 1993.
Marshall is editor of *Mediamatic* magazine, Amsterdam.
Roberge, Gaston, *Chitra Bani*, Calcutta: Chitrabani, 1974, p. 128.

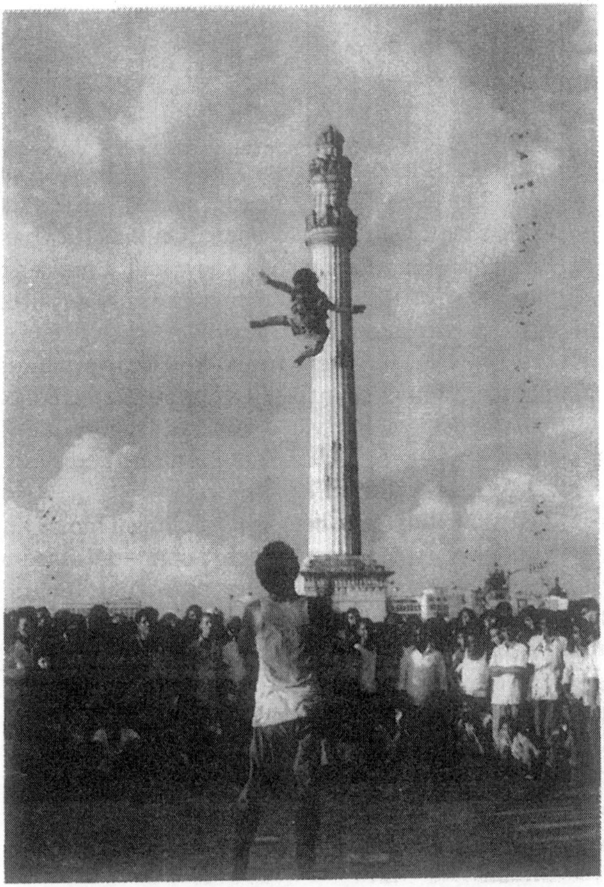

11. Each culture organises its space for public gatherings and communication in a manner characteristic of that culture.
Santanu Mitra

# 14. Disembodied Self and Virtual Sex

There is a marked difference between watching a slide show and watching a film. The movie moves, or so it seems. But the slide show does not give that impression of movement. On the other hand, there is a marked similarity between a slide show and a movie: both the spectacles simulate situations we encounter in day to day life. That is, both slide show and movie simulate "reality".

Today a third medium has been created which too produces images and simulates reality. The medium results from an interface of computer and image-making devices, like video cameras, for instance. The new medium simulates reality so well that the artifact it creates has been rightly named "virtual reality", VR for short.

There is a marked difference between watching a movie and entering into virtual reality. A film programmes your mind to imagine space, time and action in an entirely imaginative experience. But in VR your body and, thus, your mind have the sensation of being there, in the space-time simulated by VR technology. This impression is created by hooking several of your sense organs to the computer in such a way that the computer "knows" how you react and it alters its presentation accordingly.

On the other hand, there is a great similarity between movies and VR as simulators of "reality". If VR seems less interested than movies in telling stories it is because, for the time being, the simulation itself is rewarding enough.

Thus, in terms of simulation, there is a continuity from slide show technology, through cinematographic technology, all the way to VR technology. Prior to the development of the cinecamera around 1895 slide shows had achieved a high degree of sophistication in their simulation of reality. The fantasmagories of Etienne—Gaspard Robertson (1763-1837) had no less effect on their European audiences than the films of Flaherty in northern Canada, or the films of Dada Saheb Phalke in India. The advent of the cinecamera made slide show technology appear "passé" and crude. The same thing is happening today with regard to cinema: the advent of VR technology makes cinematography appear very inadequate. But in fact, the ancient slide shows, called "fantasmagoria", then the movies, and today VR achieve the same aim, namely, to so stimulate the mind as to give an impression of reality. Only, the technology to create that impression has evolved.

The old debates about cinema centred on the rapport the film image sustains with so-called "reality". It was a question of knowledge. What do we come to know when we watch a movie? Similar questions were asked concerning TV watching. Such questions arise in front of VR too. But there, it is a matter not solely of knowing but of being. We do not experience being humans today the way our ancestors did. And this new situation calls for difficult human adjustments. For, VR, along with data banks are the new environment, nature, so to say, of men, women and children. And as the environment changes, you'd expect people to change too. But that change is slow to occur.

Humans, like gods, create worlds in their own image. And, so, to start with, VR bears the characteristics of present day humans who have grown used to think of space on the Cartesian model with three axes defining 3-D, who have grown used to the unnatural split between mind and body, between nature and man, nature and culture, man and woman. VR provides an uncanny experience of disembodiment, of the body-mind split. In VR your body becomes part of the electronic apparatus, a pathway between your mind and the computer, a co-axial cable, as someone put it.

This has great significance when it comes to—and it always somehow comes to that—virtual sex, or VS. You, male or female, hook yourself on your computer with helmet, glove, magnetic ball, or mouse or such gadgetry and on request a girl of the *Playboy* magazine type appears on the screen. Your eyes desire her. The computer has noted the reaction of your eyes through tiny video cameras placed in your helmet, and the computer obliges by zooming in on the girl. You want to touch her and a "feedback force" gives your gloved hand a feel of the soft flesh. You want to be there and, an arrow, your surrogate, appears on your screen. You manipulate the arrow to come closer to the girl. Your gloved hand caresses her. Alas, there is no girl there: you are utterly alone, painfully

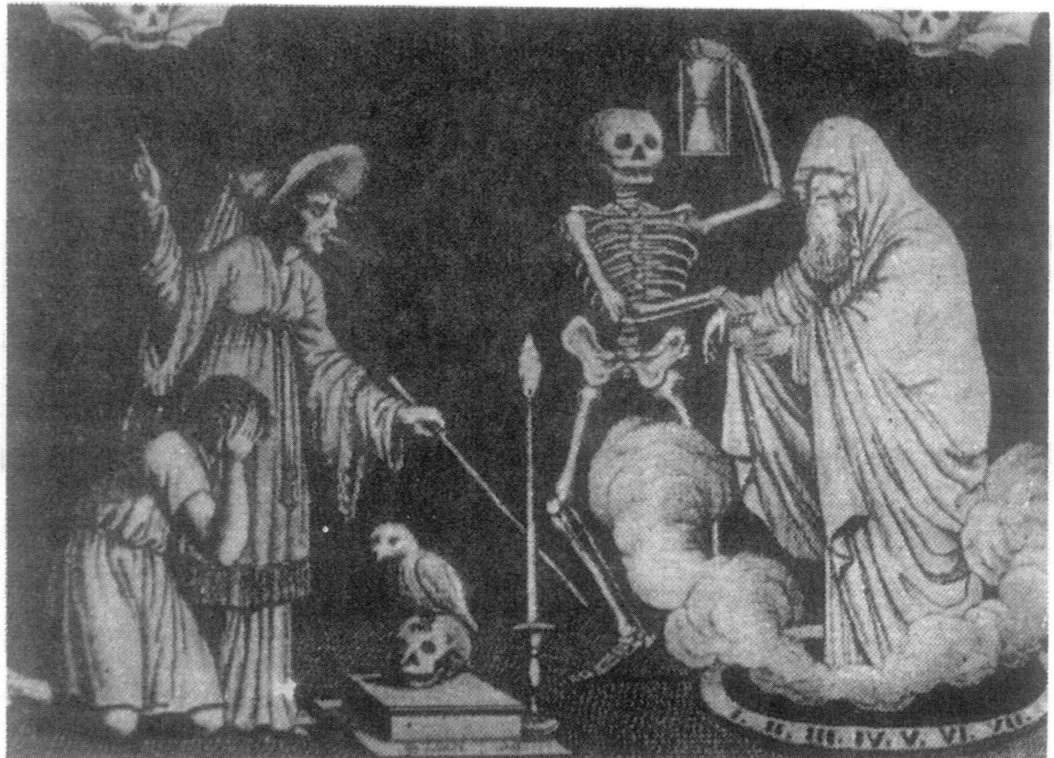

12. Virtual worlds of disembodied figures were created long before the advent of computer technology and even of cinema. This is a slide from a show of *fantasmagorie* by E.G. Robertson.

# 15. I'll Give You a Ring

Since the early 1990s telephone communication in India has vastly improved. Earlier on, saying, "I'll give you a ring" was tantamount to saying, "you won't hear from me too soon". It was taken for granted that the phone wouldn't work. In the 1970s there were plenty of jokes on the telephone in Bengali films. But from the end of the 1980s onward, films began to take the phone quite seriously, as *Ganashatru* and *Antoreen* did, for instance.

We have not yet reached the point here in India where even the most affluent people spend as much as one year of their lives on the phone. None the less, city people (above 25 per cent of the total population now and probably 30 per cent by the year 2000) use the phone more and more. With television the phone is the technology that has brought the outside world inside the home, if not yet the inside world out, thus cutting across the Tagorean divide, "the home and the world", in his novel of that name, made into a film (*Ghare Baire*, 1984) by Satyajit Ray. Hence, it is well worth pondering over the peculiarities of this mode of communication.

First and foremost is the intruding nature of telephone communication. After all, the telephone may be accessible to all, but your phone number delimits your personal estate. However, once you have a phone, you can hardly disconnect it, or refuse to answer it. Yet, there are times when you would definitely prefer not to receive any phone calls. A secretary can ward off the intruders, an answering machine is another method of self-defence. Either way, secretary or answering device, it says, "I am generally available for communication but not just now."

There may be quite valid reasons for not being available at a particular time. One may be occupied with an important business. But more often there is need for a certain mental preparation to receive a call,

# 15. I'll Give You a Ring

Since the early 1990s telephone communication in India has vastly improved. Earlier on, saying, "I'll give you a ring" was tantamount to saying, "you won't hear from me too soon". It was taken for granted that the phone wouldn't work. In the 1970s there were plenty of jokes on the telephone in Bengali films. But from the end of the 1980s onward, films began to take the phone quite seriously, as *Ganashatru* and *Antoreen* did, for instance.

We have not yet reached the point here in India where even the most affluent people spend as much as one year of their lives on the phone. None the less, city people (above 25 per cent of the total population now and probably 30 per cent by the year 2000) use the phone more and more. With television the phone is the technology that has brought the outside world inside the home, if not yet the inside world out, thus cutting across the Tagorean divide, "the home and the world", in his novel of that name, made into a film (*Ghare Baire*, 1984) by Satyajit Ray. Hence, it is well worth pondering over the peculiarities of this mode of communication.

First and foremost is the intruding nature of telephone communication. After all, the telephone may be accessible to all, but your phone number delimits your personal estate. However, once you have a phone, you can hardly disconnect it, or refuse to answer it. Yet, there are times when you would definitely prefer not to receive any phone calls. A secretary can ward off the intruders, an answering machine is another method of self-defence. Either way, secretary or answering device, it says, "I am generally available for communication but not just now."

There may be quite valid reasons for not being available at a particular time. One may be occupied with an important business. But more often there is need for a certain mental preparation to receive a call, especially when the caller expects you to take a decision. Telephone then may deprive you of the time, the context, or the information required for taking a right decision. Moreover, the phone call puts a certain undue pressure on you to decide.

There are other striking aspects of this mode of communication. The voice, isolated from the body that emits it, can reveal more than is intended because one cannot add those gestures and facial expressions that might modulate the emotional quality of the voice and give it a coloration which on its own the voice does not actually has. Film-maker Robert Bresson used the revealing character of the telephone to advantage: he liked to first speak over the phone with unknown people who wanted to act in his films. Over the phone, without seeing the person, he could feel the emotional quality of the voice of the person and to that extent of the person itself. On the other hand, the telephonic voice may not convey all that is intended. If you observe people making a phone conversation, you see them gesticulating as if to add to the voice what they feel it is not conveying. Thus the telephonic voice may express either too much or too little. That is why some people feel uncomfortable when using the phone. They unconsciously feel, perhaps, that they are not reaching out the way they would like to.

However, today the telephone line does not carry only conversations. It carries printed messages when "fax" or "telex" machines are hooked up on the line. It carries your mail in what is called electronic or E-mail through interconnected computers the world over. With a combination of cables and satellites the phone has woven a net over the whole world. Thus, not only does the phone permit instant communication from one point of the planet to another, it also hooks personal computers to what might be called a planetary computer with all its stored knowledge and its ability to create artificial or virtual worlds. Access to this planetary computer or network is a measure of a person or of a group of persons' access to the human resources available at one time. Conversely, lack of access is a measure of one's powerlessness.

A new term, TELEGEOGRAPHY, an abbreviation of "telecommunications geography", has been coined in 1990 to mean firstly, "a new branch of geography that maps the global pattern of telephone traffic and other electronic communication flows" and, above all, "the balance of telecommunication power in one country or region vis-a-vis another" (*TELEGEOGRAPHY*, 1993, p. i).

Telegeography tells us, for instance, that while at the moment there is one telephone line for two persons in affluent countries (like Australia, Canada, Denmark, France, Switzerland, USA, to name a few), in India, there is less than one line for 100 persons. If you consider that most lines are in the urban centres, this means that in some areas there may be hardly a line for several hundred people. Granted that in India we share facilities and resources more readily than is done in affluent countries (for instance, one copy of a newspaper may be read by several persons in India), none the less the difference between the number of telephone lines in affluent countries and in India is staggering.

If it were only a matter of internal communication, one could argue (not easily, though!) that India can manage with more "appropriate" technologies. But communication is not only inside India. The scarcity of lines, of fax machines and of other telecommunication gadgetry, places us at a disadvantage when we open up our "home" to the "world".

The presence of a country to the world, and thus its power, can be surmised by a comparison of its telecommunication flows, inbound and outbound. The units to compute that flow need not retain us now. It suffices to compare the figures given for different countries in 1992:

| | |
|---|---|
| USA | 9819.8 |
| Germany | 7187 |
| United Kingdom | 5638 |
| Japan | 2174.8 |
| Hong Kong | 2146 |
| Canada | 1163.5 |
| Taiwan (Republic of China) | 853.1 |
| India | 614.2 |
| Philippines | 597.9 |
| Bangladesh | 81.1 |

On the other hand, the instruments that can hook us onto the world are those very instruments that also link us together inside the country, basically the telephone lines. It would seem, therefore, that the improvement of the telephone system in India is a top priority. In a situation of so-called "under-development", however, everything has to be developed, and it is difficult to say what should come on top of the priority list. One criterion to help deciding what should come first is whether a development programme addresses issues that affect the life of the majority of the people. The development of the Indian telephone meets that criterion squarely.

## REFERENCE

Staple, George C., ed., *Telegeography 1993,* in cooperation with the International Institute of Communications (IIC), Suite 1000/1150 Connecticut Avenue, N.W., Washington, D.C., November 1993.

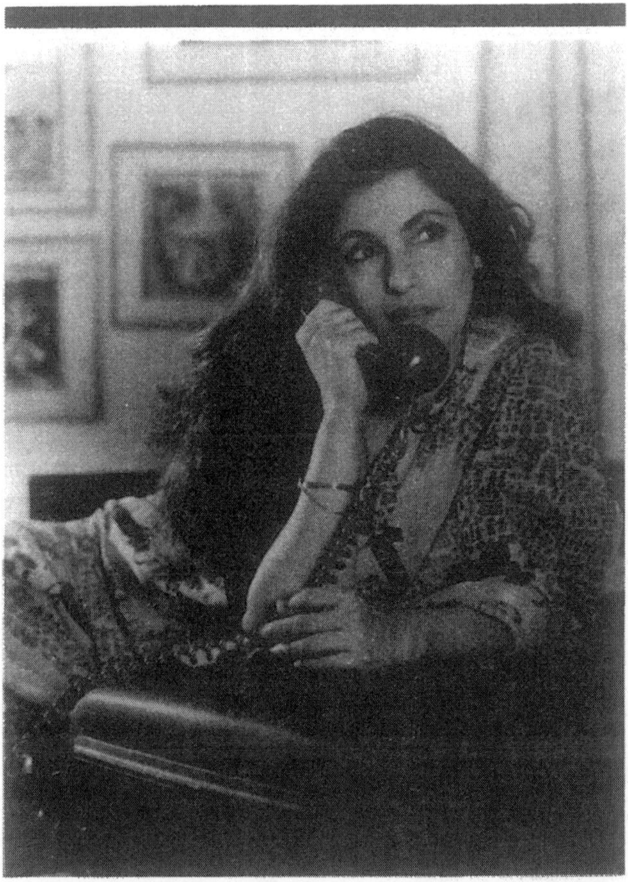

13. The telephone has always been present in the cinema. But it is only from the 1980s that the Bengali cinema began to take the telephone seriously, like in *Antoreen*, a film by Mrinal Sen. Subhas Nandy, courtesy of Mrinal Sen

# 16. Monologue on Dialogue— The Fine Art of Conversation

Everyday we spend quite an amount of time in various types of conversations. These conversations create different feelings in us—some are pleasant, others may not be so. That is because in conversation, there are people who make us feel good. These people probably do not say anything remarkable, yet they make one feel that one is special. On the contrary, some people make us feel diminished and dejected, although they perhaps do not say anything particularly disagreeable.

It should be possible to identify the factors that make one feel good in a conversation. One could then try to improve the manner in which one converses. The desire to improve one's performance in conversation may spring from the necessity of succeeding in one's job. For, all jobs involve dialogue with others. However, genuine progress can come only out of consideration for one's interlocutors. An interlocutor is a person who takes part in a dialogue or conversation. Without respect and love for others, one runs the risk of using formulas and techniques and finally of being a manipulator.

Dialogue is too important to be left solely to chance or to instinct. Hence, it is very useful to give it some thought, and to observe one's own performance. For, one cannot do without dialogue or conversation. One needs interlocutors to dialogue with. Conversely, one owes it to others to facilitate their dialogues. It is in dialogue that one grows in identity, experiences love, and becomes ever more fully a social being. But, like many of the most important aspects of human life, dialogue is at once the most common and the most unattended experience. Unfortunately it is taken for granted.

Some experts see conversation as an agonistic, that is, a combative, exercise. In their view a dialogue is a negotiation in which two opponents or players make calculated moves to win over the other. Indeed, games in which one seeks to win, may be an apt comparison for several types of dialogue, like the exchanges between a housewife and a fruit vendor, for instance. A playful verbal fight is a good analogy for those casual conversations where socialising is nothing but knocking out others and scoring points over them by means of clever repartees, jokes, disclosure of exclusive information on people and events. In agonistic dialogues the winner feels good. She might feel less so if she empathised the feelings of those she knocked out. Of course, there are conversations in which one has to fight like some interviews, for instance. But in interviews winning the dialogue may mean losing the job!

It is far more interesting to view dialogue as an encounter in which two individuals act as facilitators to each other's self-expression. There, the interlocutors do not feel the desire or the need to win. They simply enjoy transacting with each other. That makes them feel good.

A facilitator enriches the quality of conversation by giving his interlocutors the feeling that he listens to what they're saying. He does a good amount of talking, no doubt, but his speech-act is designed in such a way as to arouse the interest of the interlocutors, and thereby the participation of others in the exchange is enhanced. He is interlocutor-centred.

Five facilitating functions of the conversationalist are discussed hereafter.

## MEMORISING AND SYNTHESIZING

Your interlocutor may be improvising, she may not have had the opportunity to think over systematically what she wishes to say. The conversation may be of an exploratory nature. As a result what she says may lack clarity. There may be repetitions. Above all, she may forget important points she has made earlier in the course of the conversation. Your interlocutor will feel that she has been listened to if you summarize her points and even draw attention onto what she has said earlier. Not to contradict her, of course, but to help her not to forget that previous point.

## ALLOWING THE INTERLOCUTOR TO CHANGE HIS MIND

This is done primarily by *not* objecting to a change of mind. Some people find it objectionable whenever their interlocutors change their minds. Or else they make the interlocutor feel like a moron if he changes his mind. But many a discussion remain pointless precisely because there is no change of mind on anyone's part. At times, though, a discussion achieves a useful purpose if each participant is able to clarify his stand and formulate his statements more precisely even though no one changes his mind. The point being made here is that people should feel free to change their minds if they think such a change is called for.

## CLARIFY INTERVENTIONS

Whenever your interlocutor lacks clarity you may help him by clarifying what he said, asking whether that is what he meant. Again, the interlocutor will feel that his intervention has been listened at and indeed received. This may help him to gain confidence and be more articulate.

## TONE DOWN ANIMOSITY

Often statements carry a load of hostility, anger or animosity. This may be toned down in at least two ways. One, you repeat the statement made by the interlocutor, flattening out the edge of animosity. Two, you focus on the animosity itself by saying something like, "I seem to perceive some annoyance in what you said, did anything annoy you?" This second course may facilitate dialogue whenever some hostility can be perceived in the statements of a person.

## RELEASE TENSION

Whenever tension develops, one way to help releasing it, is to crack a joke. But it is important to know that joking is most often done at the expenses of the interlocutor. The joke may embarrass and even humiliate him. The supreme art of joking is achieved when the joker pays the cost. That is, when the joke involves the joker, not the interlocutor. Joking in conversation is a very complex manner of intervention which would require a separate treatment. This mode of communication can achieve several effects both positive and negative. Suffice it here to mention that jokes or humour used judiciously may release tension.

What happens when a facilitator meets an interlocutor of the combative type? The best course is for the facilitator to allow the interlocutor to win, without entering into a fight. But in order to allow the other to win on his own terms one must have achieved a good degree of self confidence. Above all, one must avoid entering into a mirror like relationship where one mimics the other person's behaviour, as if saying, "you are nasty, I too will be nasty". Why should one give anybody the power to determine whether one will be nice or not? Freedom implies that one decides how one behaves.

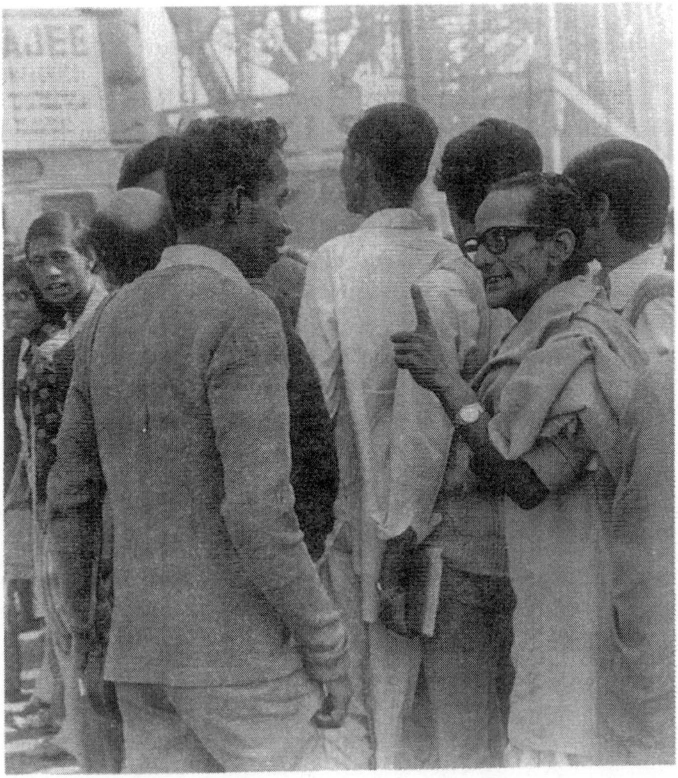

14. A conversation can be seen as an encounter in which two individuals act as facilitators to each other's self expression.
Kishore

# 17. Ego, My Brother

I am quite fascinated by a train of ants labouriously making their way, carrying particles of something I take to be food. Ants, such as these, definitely know what they are doing. Is there an obstacle? They go round it and continue on their set course. If they meet ants trailing in the opposite direction, they remain undisturbed and seem to know what the other ants are about. It's as if there was a little ego within each of them, a tiny "I" who goes its own way and knows as much as it needs to know to live its ant-life.

It would be interesting to communicate with the ants. But they are locked up, as it were, in the confines set by nature. They cannot open up to anything outside their ant world. They are immersed in the flow of life. They cannot think of themselves (so I believe) as "other" than the rest. The little "ego" I said they seem to have, is not quite an "I" who can address you as a "You".

In any case, the ants totally ignore my existence so long as I do not intrude physically into their world. And hence the question of communication with me does not arise. They have no idea that I am watching them, that I know them, that I even love them. (For, they amaze me and, in spite of their tininess, I find them in some way loveable.)

I wonder: could it be that I too, like a little ant, am the object of another being's knowledge and love and that I am not aware of it? Of course, my friends know and love me. And I know it. But they know me only to an extent. They cannot penetrate the recesses of my consciousness. On the other hand, I may be in their consciousness, but I can never occupy it fully. My question is, can there be a consciousness, larger than mine, larger than the sum of my own consciousness plus that of my friends? A consciousness in which my consciousness and theirs would exist like drops of water in the ocean?

On the basis of their experience the sage and rishis answer: "yes". They indeed affirm that there exists such a larger consciousness. And they claim that one can enter into it and indeed merge with it.

Wouldn't it be a fantastic experience for an ant if it could expand its consciousness (whatever that might be!) into mine, and, why not, into a universal, all-encompassing consciousness?

The ant cannot achieve that feat: but I can. I can, that is, if my ego, my brother, lets go. The ego, that bundle of faculties which permit me to be "me" and to function in the present world. Say, my memory, my attention, for instance. And above all my rational thoughts. All these, required as they are, bind me to the particular, the limited, the transient. And my ego clings to these bounds in sheer fear of annihilation.

The ego is absolutely required for communication. It is strange, therefore, that it should be also an obstacle to communication, not only with the wholly other, but with all the "others". How can that be? The ego is a bit of a trickster. The ego is fragile but it thinks of itself, of its diminutive self, very highly. Indeed, the ego is puffed up with "ahangkar" of its own making. The ego is a maker of "ahang".

It takes years for a human to become an ego, an "I" capable of relating to a "You". A mother talks to her child on her lap, she addresses it lovingly, and the infant soon emerges as a he or a she. The infant was part of the mother. It separates and begins the adventure of being "other". The adventure is at once terrifying and rewarding. For, "other", the ego can survive only if it has the courage to acknowledge its own otherness as well as the otherness of other egos. Two temptations: the first is to cling to the other, in a desire to merge with it, and even to disappear within it. The second temptation is to deny the otherness of the other, especially when the other is perceived as a threat.

The ego has got its feelings, the source of great joy but also of great suffering. In particular, while transacting with others the ego gets hurt. Or it hurts others. For fear of being hurt, then, the ego shrinks within itself, or else it pretends to inflate itself to limitless dimensions. Everyone knows all this only too well, only too painfully, that is.

Another problem arises when the puny ego dares, in its otherness, to face the wholly other. The experience is bewildering. At least to the mind. But to the heart? The heart, more readily than the mind (the poor thing is prone to bickering), expands to the dimensions of the "Other" The mind is bewildered by the "Other", the heart gets purified in the furnace of life.

I found my "self" on the knees of my mother when she awoke my ego.

Similarly, I find the Self when I confront the Other. But my ego, my brother, has to let go if it is to open up to the Other's dimensions. That does not mean that the ego has to disappear. But it must face the Other and allow that greater consciousness to envelop it, tenderly, fascinatingly, powerfully.

Once the ego lets go it becomes Other. For fleeting moments, perhaps. Between these moments it comes back to its own limited self. Yet, with the deep knowledge that the Other holds it within itself, infinite as the Other is. Being held by the Other helps tremendously in relating with others. Because they too, whether they "know" it or not, are wrapped up in the Self. They are parts of the Other. Rooted in the Other, the great multitude of egos cannot be at odds amongst themselves. Communication is the working out at the ego level of the communion which is the substratum of all beings.

All that is said here can only be a poor metaphor for the life experience that is open to each human being. But that experience is in many instances indefinitely postponed, as it were, by what French philosopher and mystic Pascal called "divertissement", the diversion of one's attention by every form of entertainment or wilful distraction.

By its very nature the ant is unable to communicate with me. If I do not communicate with the Other, and with others, it can only be by choice or by misfortune. The choice of an inflated ego, or the misfortune of an ignorant ego. Who, what, can deliver me from pride and ignorance? Or am I condemned to live like an ant, fully known and loved infinitely without ever knowing it?

Ego, my brother, will you not let go?

## REFERENCE

Borges, Luis, *The Circular Ruins*.

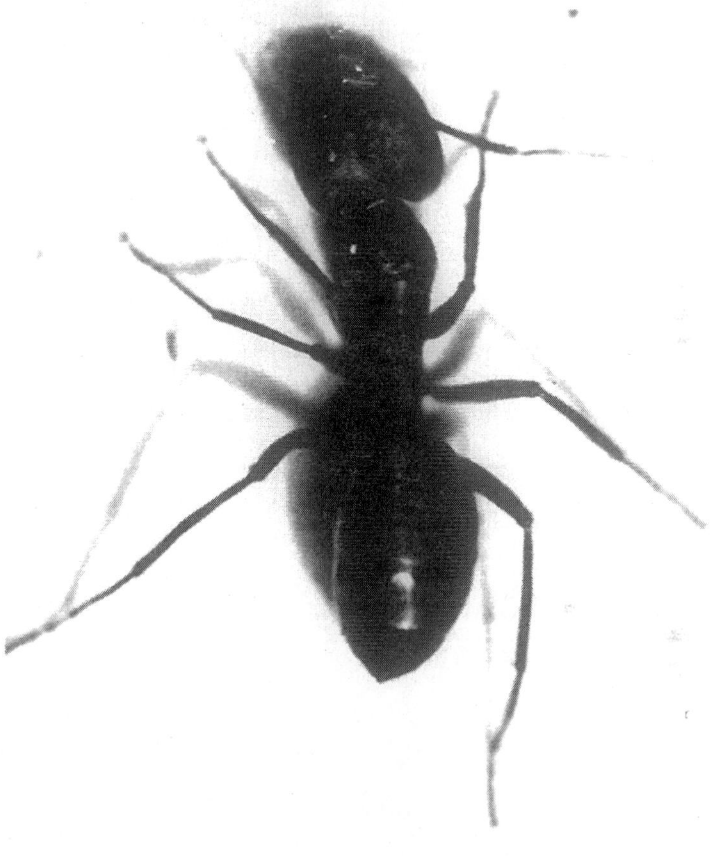

15. I wonder: can it be that I too, like a little ant, am the object of another being's knowledge and love and that I am not aware of it?
Claudin Gomes

# PART THREE

# CINEMA

# 18. The Invention of the Cinema

We are told that cinema was "invented" in 1895 and that the first cinema shows took place in that year. But there is something odd about all this.

Firstly, there are too many people making reasonable claims of having invented the cinema in or around 1895: the Lumière brothers in Paris, Thomas Alva Edison in the USA, Max and Emil Skladanowsky in Germany and William Griese-Green in England.

There is a story, probably apocryphal, that Louis Lumière, the French inventor, was working on an apparatus (the future cine camera) which would take still photographs of phases of a movement at a certain speed and then would show these still photographs at the same speed in order to create in the viewer an illusion of continuous movement. Lumière was not successful. One day, so the story goes, he had a headache and he went out for a walk. He chanced to see a woman at her sewing machine. And EUREKA! the stop-motion mechanism of the sewing machine would drive the cinecamera and the cineprojector.

Are we to assume that Edison too in New York went out for a walk to nurture a headache and saw a sewing machine? And also Green-Friese in London? In or around 1895, several people were working on a device to photograph and reproduce movement. The development of the cinecamera was a breakthrough, no doubt, but other developments were not insignificant, like the use of film as a carrier of the light sensitive emulsion instead of a piece of glass.

Indeed, the development of the cinematographic camera and simultaneously of the projector was only one in a series of technical achievements. What was special about the camera is that it made it possible to produce films industrially. Within a few years the cinema would become a mass medium.

Equating the "invention" of the cinema with the development of the cinecamera makes it possible to assign a birthday to the cinema, an important element in "history" This may appear innocent. But it isn't.

For, if the "invention" of the cinecamera was the birth of the cinema, then it follows that cinema is just a technological instrument. But cinema turns out to be an art and a language. Based on an instrument, no doubt, but much larger than the instrument itself. Ask rather, "when was cinema language invented?" A moot question.

Secondly, the cinema shows of 1895, were not the first shows of moving pictures. They were only more developed shows. Long before 1895 there had been shows of moving pictures. These shows were spectacles. And the newly born cinema was highjacked, as it were, by the tradition of spectacles.

The association of cinema's birthday with the first film shows emphasizes the fact that, whatever else cinema could have been and hardly ever was, cinema happens to be a spectacle, an entertainment and a business. Here again, cinema manages to be an art. This suggests that, after all, technology, business, entertainment and spectacle may not be as antagonistic to art as they are held to be. A refreshing thought.

By equating the birth of the cinema and the development of the cine-camera along with the first cinematographic film shows, historians have chosen to view cinema as technology and spectacle. In particular, they have made of the cine-camera a fetish, an agent, and in doing so the historians have masked the production agency of the film. This slight of hand occurs every time it is said that the camera does this or that.

"But", one can ask, "why these distortions?" Firstly, the early writers about cinema were not always highly educated persons. They were people deeply involved in the field and, consequently, they felt that they knew everything about it. Their perception of things, perhaps, was not always accurate. Secondly, they may have been influenced by the heavy publicity which the cinema business gave to its products. There was also the matter of rights on the newly developed camera. It was necessary to establish—or at least, to affirm—who developed it and who first used it.

Even as a spectacle, cinema did not have to be invented. It just grew out of Plato's cave, as it were. For Plato, the world, as perceived by man, is a spectacle of moving pictures with a highly illusionistic quality. Far from leading to a knowledge of reality, the shadows projected on the back wall of Plato's cave only give an illusion of knowing the world. But there is a difference. The man in Plato's cave does not know, until enlightenment, that he is watching mere shadows. Modern man, in the cave of a cinema hall, knows all the time that what he is watching is only a movie.

Cinema itself and cinema's history could have known a much different evolution. But from the beginning the requirements of spectacle—commercially convenient length of time, story telling, various forms of realism, etc—prevented the cinema from developing on its own. For instance, the film *Greed* (1923) originally lasted eight hours but it was reduced to the commercial length of less than two hours. Such a drastic reduction can hardly be called an editorial correction, and the resulting short version of the film is not *Greed* anymore but another film.

Some scholars have argued that the cinema was born of the desire to create a perfect duplicate of the world by means of an optically realistic image. But, in fact, the embodiment of that myth has been constantly delayed. For instance, the invention of the cinema as a technique capable of offering a duplicate of the world, was more or less complete by 1900. In that year, at the Expo in Paris, (a) short films were projected on a giant screen 21 x 15 metres in size; these films could be seen from either sides of the screen by 25,000 spectators, (b) "cineorama" was demonstrated with ten projectors and a circular screen, and (c) a 15 minute film with synchronous sound was shown. Colour was used very early by tinting the prints. Technically, from 1900 onwards there was not much left to "invent". And after one hundred years the cine-camera still works on the same principle of stop-motion. From 1900 onward, the potential of the technology to offer an illusionistic duplication of the world was not fully exploited. In that sense total cinema has not yet been invented. Perhaps the new communication technology will almost on their own make a reality of this dream.

As for the ability to create an illusion of moving pictures, it had reached a peak with the magic lantern of Etienne Gaspard Robertson nearly fifty years before the "invention" of the cinema. This ingenious showman, artist and scientist, made a picture seem to advance towards the audience or recede from them by moving a slide projector away from or towards the back of the screen. He also made the image move laterally by displacing a light source behind it. He also managed to create an illusion of movement within the picture itself. Then came cinema with the cine-camera. If we view the "invention" of the cine-camera as only one phase of a long development, then there is no reason to think that the invention of the cinema as such is over, and that there will be no further development in the technique of creating illusions of the world. But this technical development cannot be on the line of cinematography. For cinematography belongs to an age dominated by mechanical gadgets, like the train, for instance. Another technology has emerged, and with it another manner of representing the world, television. This belongs to the space age with jets and electronic gadgets.

But there is one more sense in which it can be said that the cinema has not yet been invented: instead of thinking of the cinema as a means of duplicating so-called reality, you can think of it as a language made of images that are independent of the objects they happen to look like. This use of the cinema, exemplified by film-makers Eisenstein and Godard, among a few others, has not been pursued vigorously and here too it can be said that cinema, as a language, has not been invented yet. Could not television, then, be a new step forward towards the "invention" of the cinema?

Instead of proclaiming the death of the cinema, might not one hail television as a new phase in the history of the motion pictures? No. That is not the case at all. The cine-camera had made the industrial production of images possible. But the cinema image was still the product of a specific culture. Television and the attendant cybernetic technologies have made possible the total commercialisation and globalisation of the moving images. From then on television images do not relate to specific cultures. Furthermore, the television pictures do not need to refer to what they appear to resemble to, and their "live situation" quality is a sham. Television pictures do not refer to anything except to themselves. If cinema was first a spectacle mimicking "reality", television creates "hyper-reality". The unreal is proclaimed to be more precious than the real. We are aeons away from the Vedic prayer: "*tamaso* ...". Obviously, what is said here does not apply to television in general, still less to television "as it could be", but to most TV music and most of TV advertising, that is, quite a large chunk of television. TV music and TV advert are the context of all TV and tend to give their characteristics to whatever types of programmes they are the context of.

Television is not a development of cinema, it simply is a new image-making device. There are profound differences between the two media. One cannot derive from the other. In fact, television destroys cinema, chewing its pictures to bits. People will forget *what* cinema was, will they forget that cinema *was*?

At this point, a detailed comparison of the two media would be useful. I choose, nonetheless, to first discuss cinema only. For, only a deep understanding of cinema can help one to perceive its specificity and, hence, its difference from television. I submit that the so-called "invention of the cinema" is of little importance. What is important is the discovery that is made of the cinema by individuals and by societies.

This discovery is a form of awareness. But, as we shall see, it is not just an awareness of a technology or even of an art form, it is an awareness of how the world is constructed and represented, by whom, for what purpose, and with what effect. Cinema, of course, is not the only manner of representing the world. Journalism, advertising, art, teaching in schools and universities, scientific theories, etc., all these construct and represent the world. But cinema is the most pervasive model of representations, and surely it is the most endearing.

## REFERENCES

Bellour, Raymond and Mary Lea Bandy, eds., *Jean-Luc Godard, Son + Image 1974-1991*, New York: The Museum of Modern Art, 1992.

Pennefather, Joan, "From Cinema to Virtual Reality...", in *Intermedia*, October-November 1994, Vol. 22, No. 5, pp. 28-31.

Roberge, Gaston, *Films For An Ecology of Mind, Essays on Realism in the Cinema*, Calcutta: Firma KLM Pvt. Ltd, 1978.

Sobchack, Vivian, "The Scene of the Screen: Envisioning Cinematic and Electronic 'Presence', in *Materialities of Communication*, ed. by H.U. Gumbrecht and K.L. Pfeiffer, Stanford University Press, 1994, pp. 83-106. See especially Sobchack's use of Frederic Jameson's historical moments in the "technological revolution within capital itself" (p. 89). Fredric Jameson, *Postmodernism, or, The Cultural Logic of Late Capitalism*, Verso, 1991. See Chapter 1, "The Cultural Logic of Late Capitalism" (first published 1984), pp. 1-54.

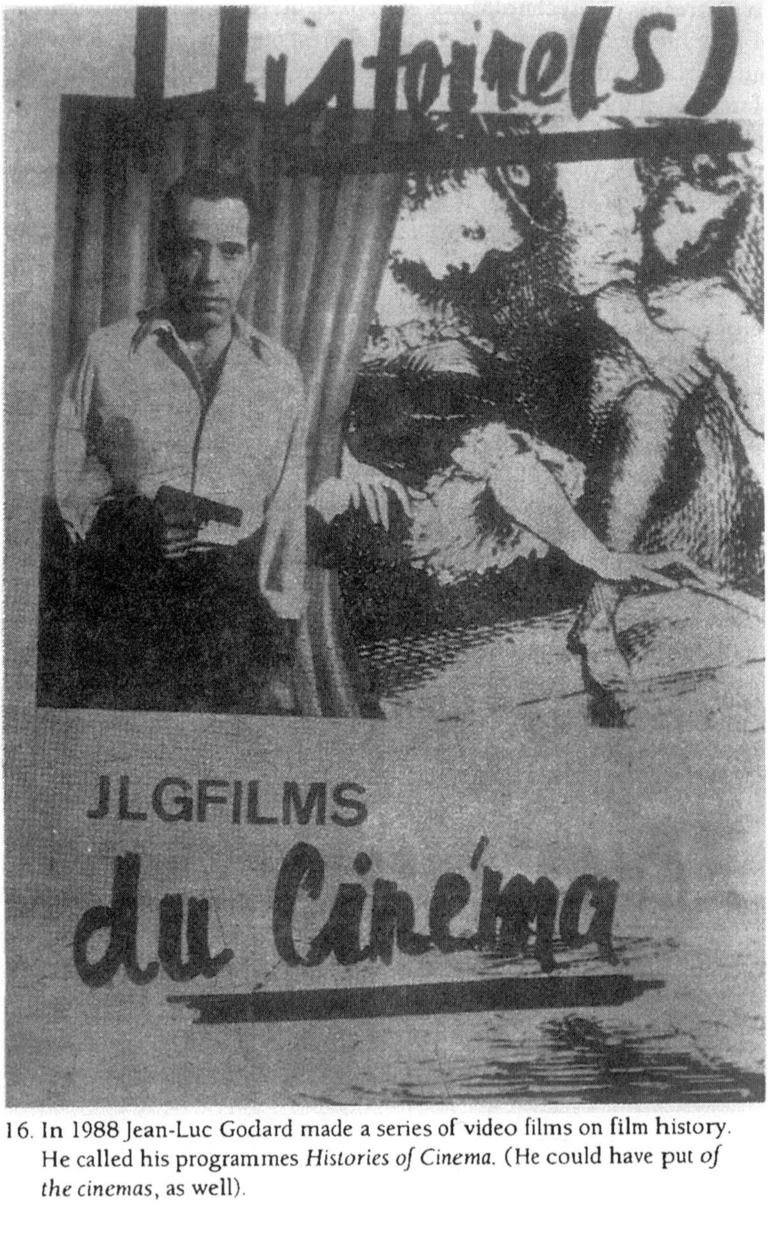


16. In 1988 Jean-Luc Godard made a series of video films on film history. He called his programmes *Histories of Cinema*. (He could have put *of the cinemas*, as well).

# 19. Cinema Awareness

Cinema is first of all a personal experience. Hence, relying mostly on my own experience and that of some students known to me, I distinguish five stages in the development of an individual's awareness of what cinema is.

## FILMS ARE FUN

The first stage is one of symbiosis. The viewer then watches movies uncritically, for the sheer pleasure they procure, a pleasure as elemental as that of feeding at the breast. It is important to note that this phase is not replaced by the subsequent phases. It remains throughout. And this is true of the next phases as well. Each phase is subsumed by the subsequent phase.

I myself lived in symbiosis with the cinema when I was a school boy. There was no TV then, but film shows were arranged every Saturday in the school I went to and most boys would attend. I do not know if we were shown anything else but I only remember the "B" Westerns, or second rate cowboy films, that were shown to us. These were serials and we came to know the protagonists quite well. In retrospect, from the few pictures that still float in my memory, I can see that the experience of watching these films had definite characteristics, of which I was, of course, totally unaware:

— The films were racist, always showing the "red Indians" as perfidious, savage, cruel, and, of course, inferior.

— They were entirely male and displayed a lot of phallic symbols, primarily guns. One scene comes to mind: the good cowboy is riding his (inevitably white) horse and, unknown to him, a bad cowboy watches from a house; then through a narrow opening in the wall of the house his gun slowly protrudes and we, kids, are yelling to warn the good cowboy of the impending danger.

— They were peopled only by thoroughly bad and thoroughly good characters.

— They were violent: all problems were solved through physical violence and use of weaponry. As the famous long faced cowboy William S. (S=Surrey but the actor preferred Shakespeare, no less!) Hart put it in a movie [*Hell's Hinges*] (1916), "Shoot first, and do your disputin' afterwards."

— They were fantasist, and perhaps that was their redeeming quality. I remember vividly: the girl friend (she was not a heroin as there were hardly any heroines in these films, only heroes) of the good cowboy had been captured by means of a lasso from the top of a cliff by the red Indians. As the girl is being slowly lifted towards the top of the cliff the good cowboy comes full speed on horseback and while riding he aims his pistol and with one shot he hits the rope which is cut by the bullet and frees the girl. But before she crashes on the ground the good cowboy has reached the cliff and he catches her in mid-air to the great discontenance of the (dumb) red Indians. Of course, fantasy never played in their favour! All of us, children, knew that this was an impossible feat, but it pleased us to believe that it happened.... Thus, we experienced the important distinction made by Aristotle over two thousand years ago between the possible and the plausible. The plausible pleases and hence is accepted as possible.

Movies then were mere fun. One was totally unaware of them as anything else than fun. But at the same time, our minds and emotions were being impressed by the White Anglo-Saxon Protestant (WASP) world view. Only later would I find that, indeed, wasps sting.

## SOME FILMS ARE MORE REWARDING

The second phase in the personal discovery of the cinema occurs when the viewer begins to find that some films are more rewarding than others. As mentioned already, the elemental, visceral, pleasure of watching movies remains, but it is complemented by some other pleasure which makes the experience more rewarding in a variety of ways.

The films that happen to be available to a particular viewer at that time of discovery are a matter of chance. In my view, it does not really matter which films are available. Year after year I have seen students moving not so much from one type of films to another type but from an indifferent to a more discerning attitude towards all films. This shift occurs upon the realisation that some films are more rewarding than others. And some such films usually are available even on the commercial circuit.

I must have been fourteen when I discovered more rewarding films. Although I was too young to be admitted in a cinema hall, I had been permitted to see the film shown that day because the person in charge knew my family. Before entering the cinema hall I did not even know what film would be shown. It happened to be *La Symphonie Pastorale* (*The Pastoral Symphony*), a film of 1949 directed by Jean Delannoy and featuring two eminent French actors, Pierre Blanchard and Michèle Morgan. This was an adaptation of a story by André Gide. And the film made me think quite seriously about certain aspects of human life. I did not understand fully these aspects, of course, but I definitely pondered over them. And I felt happy that I had seen the film.

Francois Truffaut once wrote a violent article against that type of adaptations. Even as a school boy, I knew better.

More or less at the same time, I had the opportunity to visit our local bishop with a group of other Catholic school boys to wish him "Happy Christmas". I do.not recall what prompted him to say this, but at one point he affirmed that it was a "mortal sin" to watch movies on a Sunday, the day of the Lord. I was not disturbed in the least by his saying that and I was amused when he added, "See me, for instance, I never go to the movies". I knew from experience that films offered a valuable experience —on any day of the week, including Sundays! But that encounter with the bishop was useful: it made realise that religious leaders make themselves ridiculous when they pronounce on things which are not in their field of competence.

The point is, in that phase of the discovery of the cinema, one knows that some films are rewarding and one can take a stand regarding these films and cinema in general.

## SOME FILMS ARE MORE MEANINGFUL

The third phase in the development of my awareness of the cinema started with a screening of Russian film-maker S.M. Eisenstein's *The Battleship Potemkin* (1925). The film had moved me in a way that was both new to me and very profound. Some of the images in the film haunted me vividly for over a week.

Only years afterwards did I understand that Eisenstein had selected his images and arranged them in such a way that they conveyed not so much a story as they did a discourse. In other words, Eisenstein had used cinema not just as a duplicate of the world, but as a system of images to convey ideas: he had used the medium as a language. I could not have formulated it that way at the time, but I was aware of a new use of the cinema. And I responded to it.

In this phase one discovers that cinema can be used as a language. Simultaneously one also discovers that cinema can be used as an art. Although at that time the viewer perhaps does not know what makes a film artistic, nonetheless that person can feel that some formal qualities of the film have something to do with it, as these qualities enhance the overall impact of a film.

For me, the aesthetic aspect of the cinema became palpable, if I may say, in the experience of watching Robert Bresson's *Un Condamné à Mort s'est Echappé* (*A Man Escaped*). It could have been any other film so long as it had aesthetic potential. That is why, it is important to show such films to all, but especially to the young so that early they "taste" aesthetic films and appreciate the difference.

Thus, while in the first phase, one is in symbiosis with the films one watches, and one appreciates them because they provide fun, in the second phase one takes some distance and realises that some films are more rewarding than others. In the third phase one becomes aware that cinema can be used as a language and as an art form. In this third phase films appear more meaningful.

## FILMS ARE DETERMINED BY SOCIETY

But the consciousness of films which I have described so far was contained within the narrow limits of a relationship between the viewer and the film itself. And the film was seen as an isolated object. This is but one form of consciousness. Another form of consciousness develops when one begins to realise that films do not exist in such isolation. For films appear to be isolated objects only so long as the viewer's mind maintains them that way. The fact is, everything relates to everything else. The world we live in is problematic, and films partake of this situation. They too are problematic. That is, they are part of some problem or other.

Those who think of films in isolation usually are unaware that there is at least one alternative to their way of looking. On the other hand, Eisenstein, for instance, was well aware that his film, *The Battleship Potemkin*, could be made only by a person who thought of films as moulded by the particular ways of thinking prevalent in his society. He went to great length to show that his way of putting the film together was quite different from the way American pioneer D. W. Griffith made his great films *The Birth of a Nation* (1915) and *Intolerance* (1916). Eisenstein claimed that Griffith was not alone to think the way he did and to create art the way he did. Eisenstein showed that Griffith thought the way Dickens thought and made films the way Dickens wrote.

Thus, the peculiarities of a film, in Eisenstein's view, do not depend merely on the genius of the film's maker. They depend above all on the way the society to which the film-maker belongs sees things and represents them. That is why, *The Battleship Potemkin* could never have been made by a Hollywood film-maker, whatever his genius.

In this phase of the discovery of cinema, one realises that the films one sees have been determined to a large extent by the society in which they have been produced. One further realises that the way one perceives a film is largely determined by the society one belongs to. That is why people who are not attuned to the society Eisenstein belonged to completely mis-read *The Battleship Potemkin*. The film is a direct call to the viewers, inviting them to join the Revolution, with the cry, thrice uttered, "Brothers, join us", and the mutinous sailors looking the spectators straight in the face. But "the" revolution is not in the past. It is in the "here and now" of the spectator. The spectator who does not belong to Eisenstein's society sees the film as a "hymn to the Revolution", beautifully made in five acts, but he will not hear the call of the sailors. For him, the film will be an object of well deserved admiration, but not a call to revolution. The film for him will be "a film on the Soviet Revolution".

## FILMS ARE THE FIELD WHERE SOCIAL STRUGGLE OCCURS

The film *The Battleship Potemkin* has helped my awareness of what cinema is to grow one step further. I was 18 when I first saw the film as a member of a film-club. Not only was I surprised by what appeared to me a novel way of making films, but I was disturbed. I had seen films that moved me deeply. But these films did not leave me uncomfortable the way *Potemkin* did. And I could not deal with the feeling created in me by *Potemkin*. Nor was there any one I could talk to about it. In fact, I was not aware that the particular discomfort I experienced was something I could have talked about. So, I ignored it. What was that feeling? It took me years to know.

Eisenstein himself has explained that his aim in making films was to "plough deep in the psyche of the spectator in a particular class orientation". Many films do plough deep in your psyche, Hitchcock's films, for instance. But most of the films one sees in one's own environment procure pleasure, intense emotions, but rarely discomfort or uneasiness. Eisenstein's *The Battleship Potemkin* had worked deep in my mind in "a particular class orientation". Evidently, I was not ready for this operation. And hence my discomfort.

What has to be grasped from this example, is that films do not just mirror what is happening in society. They are part of what is happening. Once a group has taken power over another group, it is necessary for the group in power to form in the mind of the dominated people the representations that justify their domination by the other group. On the other hand, it is possible to cultivate such representations in the minds of the people that are to be dominated. This is constantly happening the world over. For instance, the Gulf War. Here was a great display of military might designed to impress on the whole world that America was the unique power to reckon with after the collapse of the other super-powers. War was fought not so much in the Gulf as it was in the minds of the telespectators the world over. That people got killed in the process seems to have been of little importance to those who waged the war in comparison with the stakes of the war itself on global television. Thus, the TV reports were not so much representations of the war as they were the war itself.

In this phase one becomes acutely aware that cinema, like the other mass media, is a class medium in which the masses have no say even though they largely subsidise it.

# 20. India: From Cinema to Television Awareness

The various stages in the growth of cinema awareness in the individual, discussed in the previous chapter, can be observed in India as a whole. The history of cinema in India is almost synchronous with the history of the movement for independence: pre-independence struggle until 1947 and then efforts at de-colonisation. What strikes first in that history is the attention that the successive Governments of India—before and after Independence—have given to the cinema, an indication that they had a keen perception of the political importance of the cinema.

The number of interventions of the Government to regulate the production and exhibition of films is amazing. I mention some of the most important ones after 1913 which marks the beginning of Indian film production with *Raja Harischandra*:

| | |
|---|---|
| 1918 | Indian Cinematograph Act. The Act provided for censorship of films and licensing of cinema halls, and applied to cinema the controls already in place since the 1876 Dramatic Prevention Act. |
| 1927 | Indian Cinematograph Committee |
| 1940 | Film Advisory Board, to make and encourage the production of war-effort films |
| 1943 | Compulsory exhibition of Government approved films |
| 1948 | Films Division created |
| 1949 | Film Enquiry Committee<br>Compulsory exhibition of Government approved films |
| 1951 | Central Board of Film Censorship |
| 1952 | Cinematograph Act (to replace the 1918 Act) |
| 1955 | Children's Film Society |
| 1960 | Film Finance Corporation |

Some of the interventions of the Government were the result of group pressure on the Government. Such groups were either collaborating with the Government or using the Government machinery to promote their own interest. In either cases, the power of the Government over the cinemas was acknowledged and the legitimacy of that power was implicitly corroborated.

On the other hand, one finds little film scholarship in India. This suggests that intellectuals have not yet become aware of the place cinema occupies in their midst. Stages four and five described earlier have not yet been reached. It can be said that some action towards including film studies in colleges and universities was initiated after the late Satyajit Ray affirmed, nearly fifty years after Bela Balaaz, that it was time the Indian universities introduced cinema studies in their curriculum. That was in the mid-eighties. Not much has happened since then. And India is at least twenty years behind leading countries in the area of film studies.

The creation of the film societies in the late 1940s and their useful work to this day indicate that the awareness of the cinema as an art and as a language (stages two and three described earlier ) has grown to an extent among the educated public. But the lack of commitment of the societies to support certain films and militate against others is a sign that the intellectuals have not yet become aware of the political nature of the cinema. Some awareness of the actual role of cinema in social life has began to develop, though, if one can judge by the few articles and books that have appeared recently on the subject of the cinema as a social force.

As for the masses they are still in the blissful stage of symbiosis with the films available to them.

## NATIONAL IDENTITY AND THE CINEMAS OF INDIA

Dadasaheb Phalke, the father of the Indian cinemas, has claimed rather convincingly that the creation of an Indian film industry was his contribution to the movement towards national liberation. However, since there was no Indian national identity at the time of the movement for Independence the political leaders had to construct such an identity. For Phalke and hosts of others the Indian identity was exclusively Hindu.

Phalke may well have introduced in international cinema some forms of narrative and of representation which might be typical of at least some people in India. But it cannot be denied that he saturated his films with Hindu fundamentalism. What Phalke planted, others watered and nurtured. Religion and nationalism were cast together in film after film. Moreover, the nation was identified with the divine Mother and thus a certain ideal of the woman was cast as well. This all made for a complex representation: nation/woman/Mother. The category of the Outsider was also used to articulate the identity of those who could be considered to be Indian and those who were excluded from Indian-ship. Thus, a certain xenophobia was instilled in the films.

In retrospect, it can be seen that in seeking to create an Indian identity, the political leaders of pre-independent India while combating the British unwittingly continued the work of the British. The latter needed to make the Indians believe in a national identity. Such a belief was essential to keep the newly created India in one piece. Pre-independent Indian leaders accepted and nurtured the fiction. But that fiction worked reasonably well for them only so long as it was maintained in order to form a common front against the empire. Once India achieved Independence the notion of a national identity became more difficult to sustain.

In particular, it soon became evident that national and ethnic are not always coextensive. Nationhood has been sought by several ethnic groups in order to affirm and protect their identities. But India has hundreds of ethnic groups in addition to religious groups. Now that, the world over, the nation-state does not function too well as a political entity, one wonders about the wisdom of protecting an imaginary national identity by means of a nation-state. In the early days after Independence it may not have been easy to realize that the concept of the nation-state was elaborated in the service of the imperial ideology.

It is against this background that the presence in India of the Transnational Corporations, especially in the area of communications, thus of films as well, has to be assessed. For, there has been much concern about the Indian national identity in front of the media products that are showered on the Indian peoples. Transnationals, by nature, do not owe allegiance to any nation. They have no concern for particular cultures. The cultural products that they broadcast are meant to have appeal to all. They have no roots. The transnational companies see all individuals as potential consumers. They certainly will not strengthen any other identity. But one may well ask in the case of India, which identity? and which nation? Moreover, there is a definite possibility that preserving national identity becomes just another name for censorship pure and simple. A scholar has recently formulated the problem facing us:

> How to situate oneself in this configuration of transnational power and culture without being trapped by a deadened nativism? The return to "authenticity" is a closed route. There is nothing of the sort extant any longer in much of the world. How then to balance the transnationalization of economy and politics with the survival of local culture and history—without mummifying them with tourism and in museums—is the crucial question, for which, however, no answer has yet been found. (Miyoshi, pp. 742, 747)

## INDIAN CINEMAS IN THE TELESPHERE

No doubt, cinema and along with it Indian cinemas as we have known them are a thing of the past. However precious. Time and space are no more what they used to be. The world is interlinked like never before by means of satellites, telephones, cables, waves of all sorts interfacing with powerful computers. But there is no other space, no other time for us to live—or survive—in. And we have not yet had the time to adjust. The development of the new machines and their attendant cultures has been faster than our ability to realise what they are doing to us.

One thing, though, is clear. Empire and colonialism which had received a powerful impetus from cinema are now reigning supreme with the help of television. Over the last forty years or so, administrative and occupational colonialism, which had policed nearly 75 per cent of the earth's surface, has given way to more profitable, more efficient and, at the same time, more elusive, modes of exploitation. Nearly 120 countries have achieved so-called independence just to find that they are more than ever dependent on some other power. Since they are often unable to identify, let alone reach that power, they squabble at home on issues that have nothing to do with their state of servitude. And the local barons, perhaps aware that the nation-state is passing away never to be revived, try to appropriate whatever wealth remains available at home. The "outsider" is now inside, well entrenched through the local people dedicated to the pursuance of transnational goals. Gandhiji had seen this happening already in his time and he had strongly objected to it.

Cinema has to be seen in the context described here. It is difficult to believe that cinema's obsolete and cumbersome technology can survive. Moreover, the conditions in which films used to be seen have changed drastically with the penetration of television in the home. Thus, with the disparition of these conditions (large screen, projection, obscurity, collective viewing, cinema halls as a special place where to see films, etc.) cinema as a way of representing the world, as a way of telling stories and above all as a way of knowing the world, has become "passe".

Cinema awareness has to be extended now into television awareness. The first step in doing this will perhaps be in preserving or creating television-free spaces, even if very small, for individuals and small groups to be what they choose to be. Television, in line with globalizing forces, makes all people marginal. The hope today is in the margins. People in the margins must begin to marginalize television itself. The transnationals have shown the way: they marginalize the nation-state, but use its legal or military apparatus whenever convenient. Similarly, marginal people must maintain television on the margin of their ideological and spiritual spaces, but use television to advantage in whatever it can offer. Meanwhile television as a technology, an institution and a culture will grow. For, to judge from the technological developments in the offing, television too, perhaps, has not yet been invented. But, contrary to cinema, television will be invented. One need not fear. Television will be neither better nor worse than the humans who create and use it.

The problem facing cinema as well as television consists in the rules and assumptions of the presently-prevailing transnational corporate world market order. This is what, finally, one has to be aware of. Cinema was a great experience. That experience may provide the wisdom required to make of television too a great human experience.

## REFERENCES

Bourdieu, Pierre, *Language and Symbolic Power*, Polity Press, 1992 (includes 1981-4 articles in French), edited and introduced by John B. Thompson (1991).

Esteva, Gustavo, "A New Source of Hope: The Margins", in *Interculture*, Vol. xxvi, No. 2, Spring 1993, issue 119, pp. 2-62.

*Intermedia*, "Globalisation and National Identity", August-September 1992, Vol. 20, Nos. 4-5.

Menon, Vijay, "Tradition Meets Modernity on the Path to the Global Village", in *Intermedia*, January-February 1993, Vol. 21, No. 1, pp. 29-31.

Miyoshi, Masao, "A Borderless World? From Colonialism to Transnationalism and the Decline of the Nation-State", in *Critical Inquiry* 19 (Summer 1993), pp. 726-51.

Niranjana, Tejaswini *et al.*, eds., *Interrogating Modernity: Culture and Colonialism in India*, Calcutta: Seagull, 1993.

Rajadhyaksha, Ashish, "The Phalke Era: Conflict of Traditional Form and Modern Technology", in Niranjana, pp. 47-82.

Said, Edward W., *Culture and Imperialism*, London: Chatto & Windus, 1993.

Stix, Gary, "Domesticating Cyberspace", in *Scientific American*, Vol. 269, No. 2, August 1993, pp. 84-92.

Zutshi, Somnath, "Women, Nation and the Outsider in Contemporary Hindi Cinema", in *Niranjana*, pp. 83-142.

# 21. Innocent Pleasures in the Dark

It is difficult to think of the cinema except in terms of pleasure. But how to describe the pleasure cinema gives? To start with, one has to realise that the cinema pleasure has changed over time and will continue to do so.

Some of us have not known the so-called silent cinema. That was before 1930 when films were shown with orchestra accompaniment, or, in case of lower budget films, with the accompaniment of an electric organ. The artiste playing during the silent film gave a "live" performance which added to the pleasure of watching the movie. At times there were also people who read aloud for the benefit of those who could not read the title cards appearing during the film. They too added to the "presence" of the show.

But there are among us some who have not known the movies of the period after 1930 until the advent of television, when movies were the unchallenged entertainer. And entertain, they did. Perhaps the hundredth anniversary of the cinema is a good opportunity to reminisce on the pleasures of pre-television cinema. For, cinema will never again be what it was before TV. Accordingly, anthropology will note a mutation of sorts from movie man to "teevee" man.

First of all, you went out to the movies. You went out of your home, out of your world. You paid for the pleasure the movies promised you and more often than not actually gave you. You entered a place set aside only for cinema. For, movie theatres, in spite of the name, were hardly ever used to show theatrical performances. The cinema house was meant for movies alone. And it was quite different from your home. Some cinema houses called themselves "palaces", or in India, "mandir" And they deserved the appellation.

You took your seat and at the appointed time the lights dimmed out. The screen was uncovered and lighted up. A strain of music issuing from nowhere filled the space: you were in another world, a dark enclosure not unlike the famous cave Plato talked about. You saw shadows in front of you. But contrary to the unfortunates in Plato's cave, who were deceived by the shadows they saw on the wall, you knew that "it's only a movie", as Griffith, the father of American cinema, used to say. Yet, you loved to be taken in: you loved to believe in the ghostly characters performing in front of you. That was part of the pleasure.

But the cinema pleasure was even more basic. You absorbed the flickering images as you absorbed food. And, indeed, not rarely you brought along in the movie hall a supply of snacks. The cinema pleasure, apart from any voyeuristic pleasure, was first of all visceral. That is, Scopophilia, it is called. Munching popcorn or *chanachur*, indulging your scopophilia, you abandoned yourself to sight and sound and regressed, psychologically, quite some years back in an artificial infanthood. Though unaware of it, you felt like a child feeding at the breast of its mother. Such was the depth of the pleasure.

But the moving pictures moved along, and they moved your mind and your every emotions. You loved that. Romance, thrill, horror, sadism, violence, killing ... you loved it all. You loved to be manipulated psychically. You loved to identify with heroes, heroines, at times even with villains. For, the cinema heroism you experienced was achieved effortlessly and your vicarious villainy went unpunished. "It's only a movie." So you loved imagining yourself in situations which your natural cowardice or acquired scrupulousness made impossible for you to live in real life.

You enjoyed laughing until you could no more so much it pained. And this laughter was so refreshing. For, on the screen characters were allowed to behave according to the logic of the situation into which they were forced by life and society. Not according to the demands of good taste, decorum, or decency. And you, in the dark hall, could freely laugh at behaviours which in real life you might have disapproved of.

In the hall you were alone, but all the while you knew that a crowd of others were alone too. And thus, hundreds of anonymous viewers were alone—together. Alone, but not lonely. You were aware of people around laughing like you, sighing, pining, or fearing. Alone, you felt a part of a congregation, deeply involved like you in watching and enjoying pleasure.

You went to the movies, and it did not matter much what movie was shown. So long as it moved, it moved you. There was no television to solicit your company in the evenings. So you could go to the movies more or less frequently, more or less regularly, as you went to church, temple or mosque. You needed the comfort of these innocent pleasures in the dark at more or less regular intervals. One could not quite speak of "addiction" in your case. But an astute observer would diagnose your condition: movie man, you suffered from cinephilia. But there was no need to worry, it was of no clinical importance, so long as you could tell yourself, "it's only a movie".

These pleasures were innocent. Or so you thought. You were amused as well as comforted by the knowledge that some people, officially appointed for the purpose, had removed some of the excessive violence, some of the undue permissivity in matters of sex. For you too enjoyed "some" sex and "some" violence so long as they were not too shocking. What the censors had passed, you felt, must surely be acceptable and, therefore, enjoyable. Meanwhile, without pain you learnt a lot about how the rich become such, how the downtrodden suffer magnificently, how one looks at the female body, how law and order finally triumphs, and truth prevails. And when you left the movie palace you wondered how the so-called real world could be so dull. But not to worry, you'd again go to the movies and enjoy some more. Until you woke up and realised that so-called reality is even more enjoyable than its simulation. Not everyone agreed with you. But that did not prevent you from enjoying both the real world and its movies.

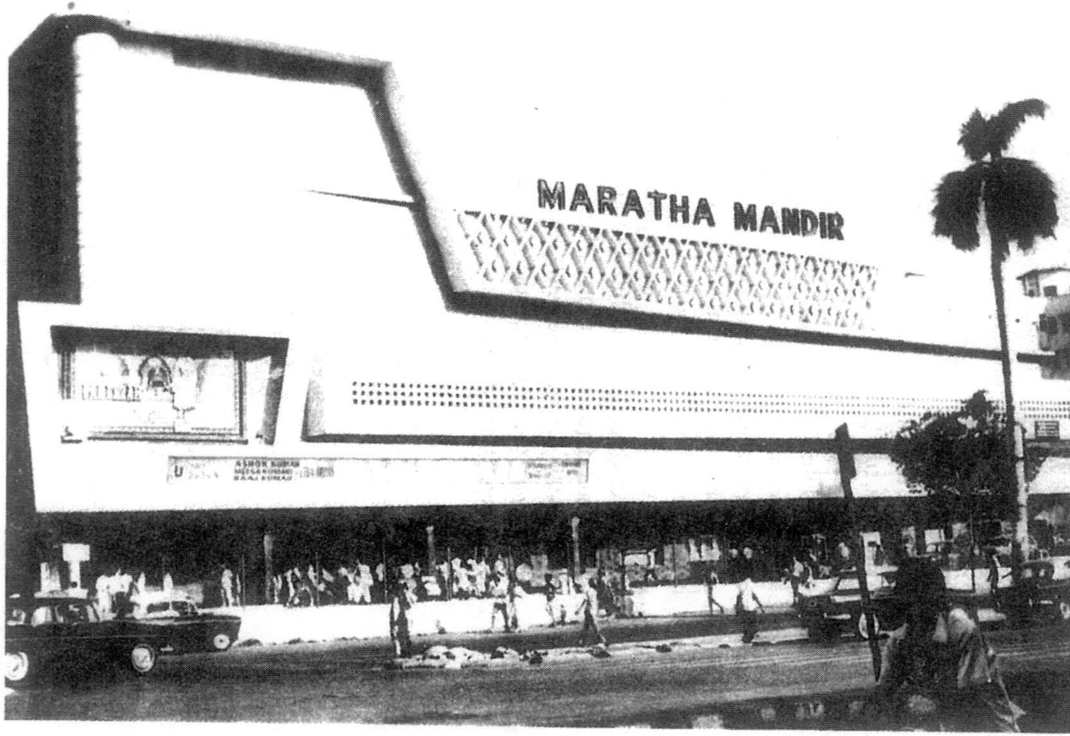


17. Some cinema houses called themselves *palaces* or, in India, *mandir*.
Gaston Roberge

# 22. Maligned, Fleeced, Yet Beloved: Cinema

We often hear that a particular film is *commercial trash, non-art, non-cinema* even though that film was literally worshipped by millions of viewers. Cinema has always been received differently by the people and by the establishment. For instance, artists had to fight to have cinema recognised as an art form. At one time religious leaders considered cinema halls as the antechambers of hell. Governments in many parts of the world, while deprecating the film entertainment, levy heavy taxes on the industry providing it. It took decades before courses in cinema studies could be offered in universities in Europe and in north-America.

India, in general, has not yet recognised cinema as an object of formal academic study. Cinema has not gained acceptance here, except as entertainment, an entertainment that is vituperated, maligned and fleeced. There is a reluctance in having cinema seen as any other thing than entertainment, as if the pleasure provided by cinema was endangered by any form of analytical thinking about the medium and its audience.

There may be individuals who hate watching movies, but the fact that millions of people consistently pay for watching movies, whether at home or in a cinema hall, enables one to say that everybody loves cinema. Then why does every possible "establishment" denigrate it?

Today, yet another powerful establishment, that responsible for "development", refuses to see the relevance of cinema. In theory, development is defined as a process leading to the free and humane existence of a person within society. However, in practice, development is framed in terms of the international market. The economic aspect of development, undoubtedly very important, has been made the sole goal and criterium of development. It is possible that, however paradoxical this may be, "materialist" West and "atheist" communism have concurred in orienting present day society in that aberrant and suicidal direction. The market, not the men and women that engage in its arena, has become the sole object of development.

Prodded by the logic of the "free market", society is unable to view the needs of human beings as objects of development, not even as relevant to development. That is why, military budgets are increased while the allocations for basic medical care and for education are cut drastically. Even though basic health services are scarce, millions of dollars are spent on pharmaceutical research. Similarly, large sums are expended on advanced "research and development" seldom meant to "develop" the products and technologies required by the poorest societies.

In that context, does not cinema appear totally irrelevant to the development process? At best, cinema is assumed to constitute an entertainment for impoverished workers, and a pastime for an "elite" that is felt to be alienated from the masses and divorced from social reality. It is as if "planners" thought it good that these two groups keep busy, the ones with their "vulgar" entertainment, and the other with their aesthetic delights. In that way, both the masses and the elites, experts seem to believe, will not interfere with the development process as planned by these experts. Meanwhile, the public, rich and poor alike, consume film after film.

There is a profound difference between a high quality film like *Agantuk*, by the late Satyajit Ray, for instance, and a popular film like *Sholay*. Yet, I would argue that both the films fulfil the same function, even if differently. And that function is to cultivate the mind of the movie goer. Ray's *Agantuk*, to expand on the same example, was his spiritual, or perhaps more accurately, his humanist testament. A statement on the present "crisis in civilisation", to paraphrase the title of the last book by Ray's model, Rabindranath Tagore. On the other hand, *Sholay* was a statement on the emergency clamped on India at the time of the film's release. The latter popular film was quite candid, while the former was consciously crafted. Both the films did not deliver the same message, obviously, but both the films dealt with contemporary "reality" and propounded views about it. For that reason, both the films deserved the serious attention of the scholar.

How were these films received? *Sholay* was nearly banned (for showing excessive physical violence! a euphemism at the time of a national emergency) and film critics wondered whether *Agantuk* was up to the earlier achievements of Satyajit Ray. What both the films had to say was of little concern to either the administration or the academics. There is a blind spot in some people's range of vision concerning culture. Millions of people have seen *Sholay* and have found the experience of watching it rewarding. That does not mean that *Sholay* is a "good" film, nor is that quality affirmed here. But when millions of people participate in a cultural event, then it is worth examining how that event has engaged the viewers. On the other hand, when one of our foremost artists delivers his testament into our hands, it is well worth pondering on what he said. The question of whether his manner of saying is up to the standards previously set by the artist is totally irrelevant. As would be irrelevant the statement that the voice of Tagore, when he read aloud his *Crisis in Civilisation,* was not as harmonious as it was when the poet was forty.

I cannot enter into a discussion of the "meaning" of the two films mentioned above. I use them solely as examples showing that cinema, by and large, is not taken seriously, except as a source of pleasure.

Tremendous efforts and funds are expended to "educate" the public, especially the illiterate masses. But little attention is given to the fact that parallelly to these numerous educational campaigns, both the illiterate and the educated are schooled in ways of thinking and ways of feeling that are either supportive or subversive of communal harmony, of respect for life, of trust in humans and in their capacity to live in society, of scales of values where economics is subordinated to other needs of men, women and children.

However, to deal with films in their full dimension, some concepts and methods are required. Skill and knowledge are best acquired in an academic environment. That is why it is so important to introduce cinema studies in universities and, at best, in colleges and schools too. Some work on those lines is being done here and there in India. But a much more vigorous response is required throughout the country if we are to begin to train some of our youths in the practical art of "reading" films.

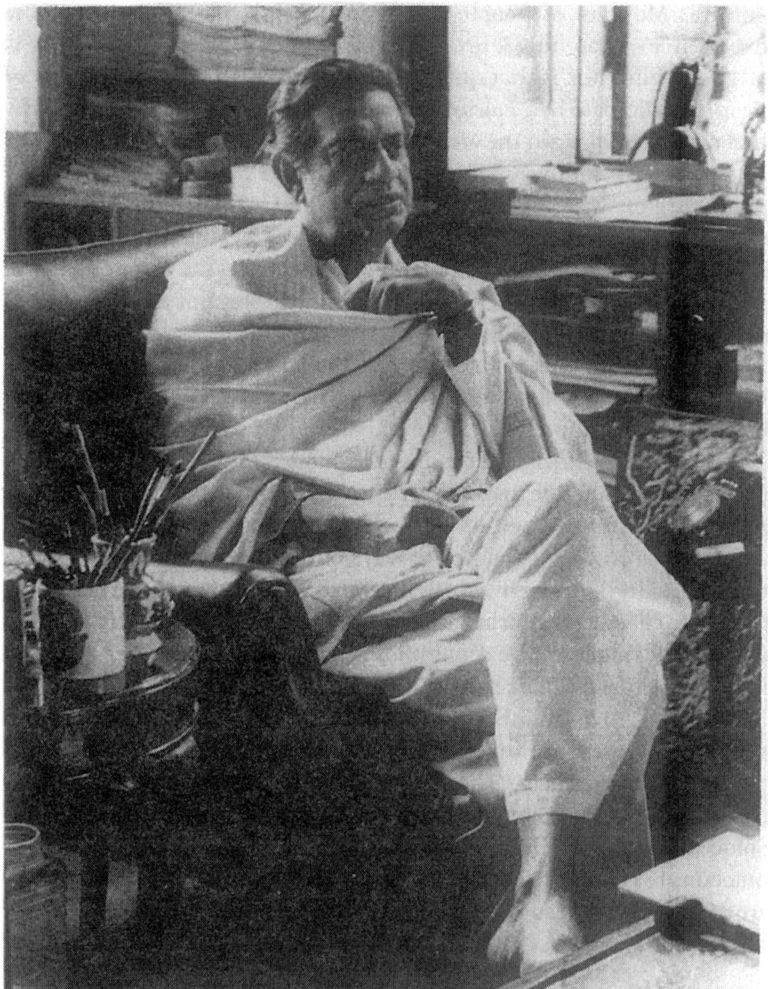

18. The late Satyajit Ray's last film, *Agantuk*, was his spiritual testament or, perhaps more accurately, his humanist testament.
Gus Beeckman, Courtesy: *Vivant Univers*

# 23. Hundred Years of Film Theory: A Panoramic View

The following panoramic view of the history of film theory, admittedly, is limited and personal. But it makes sense of several otherwise unrelated facts.

Cinema has been the object of theoretical reflection from the day it was developed. That is a curious phenomenon. For, cinema is first of all a form of entertainment. Why should it retain the attention of scholars? The answer to that question is complex. It has to do with business and technology, with pragmatism, with the thirst for understanding, and with politics.

## A. BUSINESS AND TECHNOLOGY

Cinema is not only an entertainment but also a business. Soon after cinema began, it was important to claim ownership on the new gadgetry that made the entertainment business possible. The first essay in film theory was penned in 1896 by T.A. Edison's talented assistant, William Kennedy Laurie Dickson. His piece, significantly, was titled: *History of the Photographic and Scientific Experiments and Developments Leading up to the Perfection of the Vitascope . . .* (Ramsaye, pp. 63-7). Dickson carefully used all the names that were then known to refer to the newly developed instrument, like kinematograph, vitascope, kinetograph, kinetographic stage, kinetoscopic drama, etc. That was to ensure that the rights of ownership were attributed to his employer, Thomas A. Edison. There was, at the time, a fierce battle concerning those rights between French and Americans.(The recent battle over the name to be given to the virus involved in AIDS makes it easy for us to imagine the bitterness of the fight over the cinematograph rights.)

Thus, from the beginning, thought about cinema was focused on the technical apparatus. Afterwards, cinema business continued to put emphasis on the technical aspect of the cinema. For instance, when around 1931 the industry developed the technology to record synchronous sound on the picture film, it claimed that from then on, cinema was talking. In making that claim the industry created the "silent" film. Before 1931, cinema had been anything but silent. The new development of synchronous sound obscured the fact that somehow film had always been if not talking certainly accompanied by sound. This exaggerated claim of the industry was to weigh heavily on subsequent film theory. Even today, the debate goes on with people like Jean-Luc Godard claiming that the so-called talkies destroyed the infant cinema. According to Godard, cinema language was unable to reach maturity because of the advent of the talkies. Perhaps it was better that way. Had film language fully developed before 1930, it would have had to be re-created to accommodate synchronous sound.

But cinema is not just technology: it is also a language, to quote the last sentence of Bazin's seminal essay on the "Ontology of the Photographic Image". When was cinema language "invented" or "born"? Obviously not in 1896. More likely in the late 1930s, after the "invention" of the talkies.

There is another striking feature in Dickson's piece: not only did Dickson use all the names of young cinema, but he also foresaw all the possible uses of the medium, including reports on the latest doings in Mars, Saturn and Venus by "intrepid kinematographic reporters". No wonder if Terry Ramsaye called this writing "the first psalm on the cinema", forecasting "a cosmic film industry" (Ramsaye, p. xviii).

## B. PRAGMATIC FILM THEORY

Parallelly to this trend of thought centred on technology there was the reflection of those who wondered how films achieved their effects, like telling stories, arousing emotions, and suggesting ideas. There were two main groups of thinkers then: the film-makers and the film theoreticians. American film-makers like D.W. Griffith were making dozens of films and had little leisure to think about the process of film-making. Meanwhile, the Russians, like Lev Kuleshov, having less resources and being interested in an ideological use of the medium, spent a good amount of time reflecting on the cinema. In time, Kuleshov was followed by talented film-makers who were also theoreticians,

S.M. Eisenstein, Dziga Vertov, and V. Pudovkin, among others.

The reflection of the film-makers all over the world was paralleled by different film movements, like Film D'Art, Avant-garde, Expressionism, Neo-Realism, New Wave, and the like, each lasting about five years. The manifestoes or theoretical productions accompanying these movements constituted a pragmatic theory.

Another form of pragmatic theory was the constant effort to prove that cinema is an art. This may appear strange today. The fact has to be understood in the context of the development of the arts in the West. First of all, cinema had its origins in vaudeville and circus shows. In order to reach out to a vast audience cinema had to establish itself as a "respectable" art. In order to get stories cinema had to plunder theatre and literature. Already before 1910 the great stage actress Sarah Bernhardt gave useful, if ridiculous, performances in films. Cinema had to prove itself a worthy companion of these older arts. Then, the Italian film critic R. Canudo called film the "seventh art", a name that had an immediate success. Today everybody knows that cinema is the seventh art, though few people know what the other six arts are supposed to be, namely, architecture, dance, music, painting, poetry and sculpture. Fewer people bother to think whether there might be an eighth, ninth or nth arts. Indian aesthetics is not that rigid and admits of many more arts.

But while scholars were busy attempting to prove that cinema is an art, the American Establishment, ever pragmatic, did "as if" cinema was an art. It created its own "Academy of Motion Picture Arts and Sciences" in 1928 and since then it has awarded its "Oscars" to films, setting standards for the whole world to adopt. The Academy Awards are more cherished by film-makers than any other awards, even honorary doctorates. For instance, the late Satyajit Ray felt that the "Oscar" given him was the highest tribute he had ever received for his films.

## C. PURE FILM THEORY

On the other hand, there were those who simply were amazed by the new medium and tried to understand its laws, its formative principles. Theirs was pure theory, even though it was rooted in existing films, except perhaps in the case of the theoreticians of the "idealist" school who did not mind thinking about film as it could be not so much as it was. Even then pure theory often had a deep influence on film-makers, like the writings of André Bazin, for instance.

The first exponent of "pure" theory was perhaps Hugo Münsterberg whom William James had brought from Germany to Harvard University. In 1917 Münsterberg wrote *Photoplay*, a small book which was long ignored but reads well even today. The type of reflection one finds in Münsterberg can be found also, with incredible erudition, in Jean Mitry's *Esthétique et psychologie du cinéma (Aesthetics and Psychology of the Cinema)*, a comprehensive book of 1963-5, still awaiting translation. It seems that Mitry did not know of Münsterberg's book. On the other hand, the fact that Mitry too is still largely ignored is perhaps an index of the low level of interest in "pure" theory among film theoreticians even today. The massive *Esthétique* of Mitry has been edited into one volume by Mitry's friend and disciple, Benoit Patar. That one volume edition too awaits English translation.

Some time between Münsterberg and Mitry you had the school of Etienne Souriau in France who worked towards a "filmologie", an academic discipline of film, in the 1950s. That endeavour was overtaken by the cine-politics of the mid-1960s.

## D. CINE-POLITICS

Another current of film theory was mostly inspired by marxism. It attempted to formulate disciplines called in turn cine-structuralism, cine-semiotics, and cine-semiology. The difference between that current and the Münsterberg-Mitry current is its polemical orientation. Film theory based on marxism was most often part of a political project. It is fascinating to follow the meanderings of that current.

The magazine *Cahiers du Cinéma* in France under the direction of André Bazin from the mid-forties until Bazin's death in 1958, articulated a theoretical thinking of the liberal humanist type. That thinking was inspired by the personalist philosophy of Emmanuel Mounier and the existential psychology of Jean-Paul Sartres. After Bazin's death, *Cahiers* underwent a deep ideological change and started to think 'marxist'. The British magazine *Screen* borrowed massively from the French. In particular, they translated from the French original and published articles by Christian Metz at a time when the latter was little known even in France.

Parallel to the writings in *Cahiers du Cinéma*, you had the French New Wave and later on the Godard phenomenon. Interestingly, many of the *Cahiers* writers became film-makers. This shows that, in their case at least, film theory was not divorced from film-making.

But this travail in writing and in film-making demonstrates yet another important fact: films do not only "mirror" or "reflect" the struggle for ideological dominance in a society. Films are much more: they are one of the spaces where that struggle unfolds. The viewer who watches these films innocently is drawn on the stage of the ideological struggle and becomes, perhaps unwittingly, an actor or a victim of that struggle. Or else the viewer enters the struggle with full awareness of the issues at stake.

## CONCLUSION: MORE THEORY

It is not surprising that cinema should play such an important role in the life of societies: for cinema is a collective dream. Society has the apparatus to create and to project that dream. And the members of that same society enter the dream. For the time of the film and, often, much longer afterwards, their minds are programmed on certain lines that either re-inforce the power structure prevailing in that society, or question it and seek to subvert it.

This explains why cinema is kept under such tight control. Control is twofold. Official censorship of the State, on the one hand and, on the other hand, self control exercised by the film industry itself. But the two forms of control are in the same hands and serve the same interests. Although large sums of money are involved, the State does not have to interfere much, because the industry itself does not allow films to become liabilities. In practice, the industry does not take any risks on films that efficiently question society. (A degree of questioning, of course, is fashionable and sells well.) So, the State can limit itself to matters of "sex and violence" in films, thus drawing the attention of the public away from what really matters, namely, the world vision films offer.

Film critics can be relied upon to add to that diversion with considerations of "taste".

## REFERENCES

Bellour, Raymond and Mary Lea Baudy, *Jean-Luc Godard, Son + image 1974-1991*, New York: The Museum of Modern Art, 1992, pp. 159-67.

Ramsaye, Terry, *A Million and One Nights, a history of the motion picture* (1926), London: Frank & Co, 1964, Chapter 20, and Gaston Roberge, *Films for an Ecology of Mind, Essays on realism in the cinema*, Calcutta: Firma KLM Private Limited, 1978.

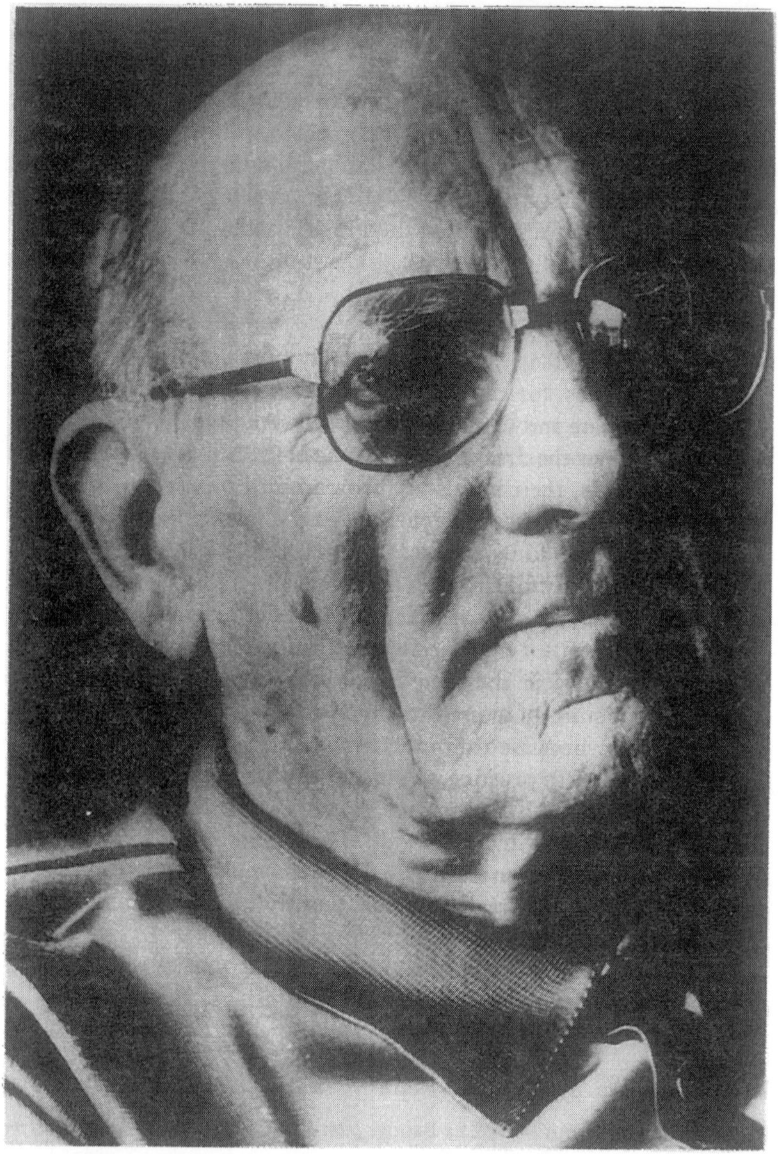

19. Jean Mitry (1907-88) and the cinema were born almost at the same time. Mitry spent all his life studying the new art, making some experimental films, teaching about film and writing numerous books on film. Yet, for various reasons, he did not get a fair hearing ... film theory is the poorer for that neglect.
Courtesy: Mrs Jean Mitry

# 24. Happy Centenary Feast Indian Cinema! May You Rest in Peace

*The birth of television has ruined all the cinemas of Europe* ( J.L. Godard). And it is about to ruin all the cinemas of India. A sobering thought as we celebrate cinema's centenary. Long live cinema, cinema is dead. Yet, cinema will not be dismissed or forgotten here anymore than there. For India has produced thousands of films and these films fulfil a vital function in the life of the Indian people. But how to encompass in a bird's eyeview such a large and diverse landscape, with so many monumental landmarks?

***

Let us think of the Indian cinema as made up of Indian films, of course, but also of the foreign films shown or made in India. Let us think of this huge collection of moving pictures as an immense, computerised, video centre, providing instant access to every film made, every film screened in India since the first film shows in Bombay on 7 July 1896.

You just skim at high speed and what do you see? It is as if the collective psyche of 800 million people opened up for you. Certain films meet with the enthusiastic response of millions of viewers, reflecting the state of mind of these people at a particular time. Other films, like precious stones amidst the glittering lore, are appreciated by only a few. The detached observer notices particular films according, of course, to his (mine in this case!) own concerns.

As you look through you meet with films in almost all major Indian languages. Your computer informs you, though, that of the silent films only about 18 hours have been preserved. A pity. Because films were most eloquent when they were supposedly silent.

And if you can retrieve erased files, you get all the censorship cuts. You are amused by the British obsession with their own image. But, as the British would say with understandable national pride, "noblesse oblige" and "honni soit qui mal y pense". But when India at last took over the scissors, she cut out scenes of violence (at times so exaggerated as to be funny) and scenes of 'excessive' sex. The virtue of India's people, so it was felt, had to be protected.

Press the button. And you get all these films sent to foreign festivals. Some are excellent by any standard. And it is fashionable, in Europe especially, to hope to counter colonialism by promoting Asian films. However, most of these films do not fare too well at home. Mostly because they are not exhibited. Ask your computer how many people in Bengal have seen most of the films by Satyajit Ray. The computer will blink with discomfort and signal "data not found".

On the other hand, the films of Satyajit Ray always appear on top of the list whenever you ask for particular types of films: children's films, historical films, biggest regional box office hits, art films, popular films, detective films, love stories, religion, modernity, woman, civilisation....

Are you in sympathy with the feminist movement? There are films for you to ponder over from Mehboob Khan's *Sister* and *Aurat* (*Woman*), 1940, to his most popular *Mother India*, 1957, and to films of the early 1990s like *Hafta Bandh*, 1991, *Prahaar*, 1991, and *Vishwatmaa*, 1992. The heroin of *Mother India* stepped out of her movie and entered the Indian Parliament. She objected to the depiction of poverty in *Pather Panchali*, untroubled by the image of the woman which she herself immortalised in the Indian psyche.

And do you look for approved information about India? The Films Division has weaved an endless tapestry authenticated by the voice of God (Pratap Sharma's). But cinema exhibitors have little concern for official "reality", and they resent being obliged to show these documentaries and newsreels.

What is, you might ask the computer, the most often depicted theme? Most likely, you will be given a list of hundreds of films dealing with vengeance. A good example of the theme? *Sholay*.

And what about the demi-gods of the cinema? These ideal men and women that have mobilised the love of millions and continue to haunt their imaginations in each regional cinema? In Bengal, one immediately thinks of Uttam Kumar and Suchitra Sen and, closer to us, a giant all of his own, Utpal Dutta. So many movie stars join politics. Of all sorts—party politics or activism. It is as if the Indian screen was diaphanous and the movie stars were projected into the real world. A unique phenomenon.

Stars pass from one world into the other and back into ... reality? dream? Your computer seems at a loss to define which is which.

***

As you scan cinema, there are sparks of vitality, of freshness: films by the unique Jean-Luc Godard. Their influence on the Indian films was felt at the time of Mrinal Sen's *Interview*, 1970, and Satyajit Ray's *Pratidwandi*, 1970. The interest in Godard is still alive today, more than is acknowledged. But the actual influence of his films was but a passing phase, no doubt proving Godard right: cinema as a visual medium was never allowed to find its own language. That is because everywhere cinema was made into a spectacle. And the requirements of spectacle are stringent, although they vary from place to place. In India cinema had to accommodate a long tradition of entertainment where the goal was to enjoy various emotions and moods. A rigorous organisation of the spectacle was not the primary concern. While that tradition has endured in the Indian cinema to this day, the films of Satyajit Ray and of several others have shown that the Indian cinema can integrate Indian arts in a highly disciplined spectacle.

***

In 1910 it was not Lumière's *The Arrival of a Train*, this symbol of Western industrialisation, which kindled the imagination of Phalke, the father of the Indian cinema, but *The Life of Christ*. That American film caused Phalke to fantasy the myriad Gods of India, Shri Krishna, Shri Ramchandra, their Gokul and—already?—Ayodhya! What he fantasied, Phalke soon projected.

By 1970 already India was recognised as the largest producer of feature films in the world, with 400 films released in that year. Twenty years later production had soared to about a thousand films a year. Now, every timeless year, India can tell stories of dream and escape one thousand and one nights. However, the population has reached nearly 800 million people. This means that every year India produces one film for every 800,000 of her people. Is India, then, the largest producer of films?

These films have been one of the strongest influences in schooling the masses. The dream of Phalke came to be true: for nearly a century, the sons of India have been able to see Indian images on the screen. These images have provided a social conscience, they have nurtured the people's aspirations, they have exalted certain values. If Indian movie stars shine both on the silver screen and in golden politics, the Indian masses enter the films they watch and step out the other side of the screen into their reality, programmed, as it were, by the dreams which the films gave them.

The early preoccupation of the India cinema with defining the nation and with fashioning an image of ideal womanhood is still at work in the films of the 1990s. These films play an important political role in nurturing in the masses an ideology which they are able to identify and see in action in particular political parties. It has been argued that the popular cinema, often termed "all-India film", has fostered in audiences a negative attitude towards change. This might help to explain why cinema and politics so often merge in India.

But foreign films too have been shown in India. What is more, foreign films have been made in India. For India is beautiful and photogenic. Above all India is "other". An "other" which the West needs to define itself. 1926 saw *The Light of Asia*, a life of Buddha. Fast forward a little and you have *Bengali Night*, *A Passage to India*, *Gandhi* (a subject which is perhaps the most precious treasure of modern India), and a detestable film, *The City of Joy*. These films too have had their influence on the Indian cinema-goers. ■

Because the Indian public loves films so intently the newly commercialised television draws this audience to itself by showing them movie films and by making a plethora of programmes from fragments of earlier films. At the same time television offers the same audience its own fare, with its own dreams, politics and values. But television isn't art, it's culture, commerce and broadcasting. Films will soon become less and less required to goad the audience into watching television.

And then films will disappear from television. It's as well, they don't belong there.

SEARCH. RANDOM.

NANDAN. FESTIVALS. NFAI. FTII. 1993, FELLINI. 8 1/2. *NAYAK*. SATYAJIT RAY. TAGORE. *CRISIS IN CIVILISATION*. *AGANTUK*. *THE BISON*. UTPAL DUTTA. FILM STAR. STAR TV. ZEE TV —

SYSTEM FAILURE. type MANIKDA.

Exit INDIAN CINEMA (Y/N) ? N   Blink. Blink. Blink.

# 25. On Manikda's 1994 Birthday

Birth anniversaries are privileged moments to remember lost beloved ones. But I hardly need such occasions to remember Manikda (Satyajit Ray). I think of him daily. I have three pictures of him, on three different walls, in my office, where I spend the major part of my days. Shahjahan had arranged a set of mirrors in a room so that in whatever direction he looked he could always see the Taj Mahal. Similarly whatever side I turn, I see an image of Manikda. And in my more pensive moments I hear the last words he had for me when I took leave from him, "Bhalo laglo"

I too say, "Manikda, bhalo laglo". I liked to be with him. I used to visit Manikda twice a month, always on a Sunday, in the morning, at the same time. These regular visits reminded me of the novel *The Little Prince* by Saint-Exupery. In the novel, a fox once told the little prince, "If you are to come to me, always come on the same day of the week. In that way I can look forward to your visits." In fact, it was for convenience that I visited Manikda on Sunday mornings. Of the two of us, who was the fox, who was the prince? I do not know. But I found that I, at least, came to look forward to my next visit. It isn't that we talked of profound subjects always. But always, whatever we talked about, he had a profound impact on me.

For instance, one day I mentioned to him that there was a plan to make a feature film on Mother Teresa. Unfortunately, some sisters close to Mother prevailed upon her, and she refused permission to have the film made. One argument put forward by the sisters was, "How can you make a feature film on Mother even as she is alive.?" I was telling Manikda that so-called documentaries are fictional too. And I felt it was better to make a film on Mother when she was alive for, after she leaves us, it will be difficult to anchor in actual facts the myths that will very soon mushroom about her. In that context I mentioned the film *Monsieur Vincent*. And I was surprised to find that the film was well known to Manikda.

*Monsieur Vincent* is a French film of 1947. It is about Vincent de Paul (1581-1660), a pioneer of social work and a favourite Catholic saint. When Manikda saw my surprise at his knowing that film, he added to my delight saying "Yes, it was a remarkable film, with an extraordinary performance by Pierre Fresnay. The script was by Jean Annouilh, and a fantastic camera work by Claude Renoir." I asked Manikda if he had seen the film recently, but he told me that he had seen it in the early days of the film societies around 1950, namely, some forty years before. I thought that anyone who could remember a 1947 French film in such details must somehow be a special person. I am French speaking and I had forgotten who the script writer and who the camera person were. But then, I am not a film-maker . . . and I am not Satyajit Ray.

There were other such occasions when Manikda showed that he was a special person. Two come to mind. Our Chitrabani team had made an animation film out of some two hundred still photographs of slum children. The film is called *A Portrait of the Pilkhana Child*. I requested Manikda to see the film and he accepted. So, Brian Balen, the film's maker, and myself showed him the film in his flat on Bishop Lefroy Road. He had very kind words about the film, but he said that a part of the music, which he liked as music, was not quite appropriate where it was used in the film. He felt that the mood was slightly wrong. We asked him which part of the film he was referring to. He answered, "I don't remember exactly which part of the film it was, but I can whistle the tune for you." And he did whistle the tune accurately. We were dumbfounded and thought, "How can a person see a twenty minute film for the first time and be able to whistle the tune of its music?"

The other incident which comes to mind has to do not so much with the culture or talent of Manikda, as it has with his greatness as a person. That incident occurred in the early 1970s. I had to be absent from Calcutta for nearly a year. And although the organisation which I head, Chitrabani, was then very small, I needed someone to replace me during my absence. I found a young man, let us call him Rajan, and I gave him the job. When I came back, that Rajan had already left for the USA where he had got enrolled in a university. I was told by my secretary who served him during my absence that Rajan had sent him to Satyajit Ray whom neither the secretary nor Rajan had ever met. The secretary was to ask Ray for a recommendation for Rajan. Apparently, it did not occur to Rajan that propriety demanded that he personally went to Satyajit Ray with his request. Upon hearing the secretary, Ray asked him in his deep voice, "Do I know the gentleman?" The secretary missed the gentle yet obvious irony of the question and said that Ray did not know Rajan but he knew Fr. Roberge whom Rajan was temporarily replacing. On hearing this Ray immediately wrote a note of recommendation for Rajan. The "gentleman" was admitted in a university. When I heard about this incident I was absolutely appalled. I felt that only a great person could be unshaken by the smallness of the impropriety. At the same time I loved Manikda for lending Rajan the immense prestige of his name just because he was replacing me.

Towards the end of Manikda's illness it had become obvious that he would not be with us for much longer. So, his departure was no surprise. Yet, I had not anticipated that the sense of loss I was to experience would be so profound and so pervasive. Manikda was such a towering personality, and he exercised such a unique influence that when he left, a void was created which is filled, to an extent, only by our fond memory of him. But there is yet another way to fill in the void: it is to strive to fulfil the expectations which Manikda nurtured and fostered regarding film culture.

Not so long ago, in 1990, he had written a note for the students enrolled in the Chitrabani Film Studies course in which he had these words: "I find it most heartening that such an event (the film course) has taken place. I have been hoping for a long time that something concrete should be done about the dissemination of film culture among the young people in our country. This course is surely a step in that direction. I hope that the enterprise will continue" (29/4/90). The enterprise continues and, in fact, the cause of film culture has been taken up by other organisations and individuals too. On Manikda's 1994 Birthday, "I find it most heartening . . . ".

# 26. A Film Festival, What For and For Whom?

Our international film festivals are believed to have two objectives: (a) to usher our films on the international market and (b) to provide an opportunity to our people to see films from outside India. Thus, a commercial and a cultural objectives.

I leave it to film-makers and to business persons to decide whether Indian films are actually marketed through our Indian film festivals. As for the other objective, namely, to give people a chance to see films from abroad, it is clear that it is not fulfilled at all. From the point of view of this second objective the Indian international film festivals are a sheer waste of money. I suggest, therefore, that the two objectives be dissociated. And two types of film festivals be held. These two types might be called the commercial and the public film festivals.

Let there be a commercial film festival aiming solely at selling Indian films on the international market. Let this be a purely commercial venture with no pretense of promoting "film appreciation". Let that type of film festival be held every year in the same city so that progressively the necessary infrastructure is developed and the organisers gain experience. Let these film festivals be competitive because awards add to the market value of films and encourage both film-makers and film producers.

However, in addition to the commercial film festival another type of festival, namely, a public film festival, is required so that our people have access to international cinema. Such access should not be the privilege of a few, specialists or not, but the right of any person wanting to know what's going on in the world.

In my view, every year there should be a public film festival in some twenty cities and towns of the country. Only about ten foreign films should be shown every year , the same films in all the cities where the festival is held. Each of these films should be shown several times so that a maximum number of people get the chance to see them.

The public film festivals should become part of the cultural life of our cities and, hence, they should not be glamorised, nor should they be competitive. Indian films have to be promoted in India too, but obviously not by means of an Indian "international" film festival. This issue is not discussed here.

The future of the cinema depends on the awareness people have of the place cinema occupies in social life. And even if in the near future cinema was to disappear altogether, the awareness people have of the cinema as a social force will extend to television. But unless people have a chance to develop a mature understanding of cinema's social function they will be unable to face the challenge thrown to them by the spread of television and video tape players.

Unfortunately, although India produces a large number of films every year, she has not yet produced a significant body of reflection on the cinema. This places India at a great disadvantage when she has to make out what television is and can be for her people.

It is likely that film technology will not be found useful much longer, and it is already a fact that the conditions in which cinema films used to be seen do not exist any more. At least in Calcutta cinema houses have become very unconformable and people who can afford it prefer to watch movies at home on video tape even though they know that they do not get the whole film experience on the small screen. In addition, today important films come to people's homes through television. So, you used to go out to see a film, now through television or the video tape films come to you in an altogether different environment. For, in the obscurity of the cinema hall one watched films intently and singlemindedly. Now, in the home, one can attend to other things while watching movies.

But before we dismiss cinema as an obsolete art form, we should wonder whether cinema has been allowed to develop its full potential. A creative film-maker like Jean-Luc Godard, for instance, doubts that cinema really grew to what it could have become. Is it too late now to allow cinema to develop? We, who are so proud of our technological prowess, should bear in mind that already in the year 1900 in Paris the Lumiere brothers held cinema shows which could be watched by some 25000 people at the same time. It seems that we have lost both the will to share cinema with the masses and the creativity to find means of doing so.

Every year, on the occasion of the film festival, shows for immense crowds of people could be organised, at least in the great metropolis of India. In addition, the same films could be made available in video cassettes for screening throughout the country. These screenings could be prepared long in advance by publicity. A context would thus be created for the screenings. The organisers of the festival would prepare notes and guidelines for discussion. The film societies could play an important role in fostering understanding and appreciation of these films.

Obviously, I am not proposing here a whole scheme, with its organisational details all worked out, but only the lines on which useful film festivals could be organised. Unless such or similar activities take place our people will not develop the media literacy which they need to live freely and meaningfully in this communication world. They should neither be swept by television nor frightened by it. After all, around 1910, shortly after it became a mass entertainment, cinema was vituperated by some well meaning preachers who called cinema halls the antechambers of hell. Yet, already in those years, and constantly ever since countless films of great human value have been made and appreciated by millions of people the world over. Cinema, perhaps, will give yet more masterpieces and television, surely, will give as great works as cinema ever did. And television watchers will not be prevented from going to heaven if they choose to go there notwithstanding preachers of whatever garb or persuasion.

# 27. Film Criticism

"Why do film critics write at all? What do they try to achieve?" Indeed, some of them seem concerned solely with showing their cleverness by tearing down the films they write about. Film-makers, of course, do not take critics very seriously. Still, critics do exert some influence on the fate of movies. For, the critics' comments are endowed with the authority of the printed word. What's good enough to be printed in a newspaper, it is assumed, must be good somehow.

I suggest that the function of a film critic is twofold. On the one hand, he informs the public about forthcoming films, their themes and their cinematic qualities. This part of the function is related to publicity but it already involves evaluative judgments. Some critical pieces must be limited to this much due to the particular requirements of the paper for which they are written. On the other hand, when longer pieces are admissible, the critic provides useful comments on the context of the film, its possible significance at the time of reviewing, and explanations of the critic's judgments. All of this must be brief, in a simple language devoid of specialised jargon and, if talent permits, the piece should be highly readable, even entertaining. Unfortunately, critics tend to be entertaining at the expense of the film's makers, and newspaper editors tend to be satisfied if the piece is entertaining, whatever its critical value.

The critic's job is not easy, the environment rarely supportive. Yet, whenever film critics fulfil their function, they greatly help both the public and the film-makers. In fact, a film critic should be an adjuvant of the film-maker, helping the latter to communicate with the public.

However, there are several types of films, from art films to so-called "commercial trash". And film criticism is concerned with all these films. A particular critic may not be able to handle all types of films, but critics as a whole, that is, the profession, should be able to handle all the films that are shown where the critics function. The poverty of film criticism as a profession in India is indicated by the fact that critics as a whole are unable to deal with several films that are important, either because the public has responded massively to them, or because of other external reasons.

For instance, in the period from the late nineteen eighties to the beginning of the nineties, say, in about six to seven years, critics as a whole have proved unable to deal adequately with the last films of Satyajit Ray, especially *Ganashatru*, but also *Shakha Proshakha* and *Agantuk*. Moreover, the same critics were unable to say anything interesting about the extremely popular film *Beder Meye Josna*, and about the execrable film *The City of Joy*. This means that critics have failed to deal satisfactorily with both high brow and low brow films. The critical logorrhea caused in January 1994 by the film festival virus did not do the profession very proud. How could a critic, for instance, write 550 words on *Heaven and Earth*, a film shown during the festival, without denouncing the absolute obscenity of that American film. *Heaven and Earth* depicts in detail how all the parties involved in the Vietnam War raped brave girls, and then the film goes on telling the Vietnamese people that they should take the war in their stride with forbearance. Committed critics should have protested against that film. Yet, we were told by the same reviewer that the film gets high marks for production value. Thank you for the information.

Film criticism is nurtured by film scholarship. However, Indian film scholarship is in its infancy, lagging far behind film production. For, India produces films that are much better than what is written about them. Furthermore, it can be hoped that the cumulative effect of the work done by the film societies, the Film and Television Institute of India, the National Film Archive of India and the various academic institutions that are taking up cinema studies as a serious discipline will yield its fruits in the near future.

But film criticism is only one aspect of media and cultural criticism. Our inability to cope with films is an index of our inability to cope with the media in general and with their impact on culture. Example: the Michael Jackson phenomenon. You met with the most radically opposed views about the star. Some were antagonistic mostly because Jackson was associated with a multinational company. Others felt that Jackson is talented and should be received as an artist even though his tour was a commercial venture. But very few were able to enlighten the readers about the values fostered by Michael Jackson, and about how parents, for instance, might relate with their children in this respect. To reduce the Michael Jackson phenomenon to a matter of national pride or of politics is to render a disservice to the public. After all, Michael Jackson does not need a tour—however dangerous!—in order to be present in India. Michael Jackson is here.

It is difficult for most of us to be aware of the rapid and profound transformation of the world in which we live. The Gulf War which we have come to know about almost entirely through television was a demonstration of the fact that now wars occur in outer space—real or artificial. But with real effects. Thanks to the media of communication, colonizers do not have to burden themselves with residing in the colonized territories and with administrating them. Furthermore, colonizers themselves do not have to occupy a specific place. Thus, today a political movement like QUIT INDIA is not thinkable. For, the masters of the "empire" are not here. Nor can we locate them. Nor can we close our "space" to them. For the communication waves need no passport to travel. They ignore borders and territorial limits. And they cannot be contained.

Cinema is an important, though limited, part of the media world. A better knowledge and understanding of the cinema can help in understanding the media world, in fact, in understanding the world.

# 28. The Documentary Film as a Voice of Dissent?

The phrase *documentary film* designates a very large group of very different films. What these films have in common is their claim to bear a special relationship with *reality*. In film literature terms like *short, non-fiction, direct, engagé, committed, vérité* alternate with the term *documentary* to indicate the particular nature and role of that type of film. The present essay, though, does not deal with this entire and rather complicated issue. It discusses only those documentary films that voice dissent. Not all documentary films voice dissent, of course, but quite a few do.

From the beginning of the cinema, there have been film-makers everywhere in the world, including India, who have used the medium to probe specific events, to voice concern, to dissent. This particular use of film is rather surprising. For, film is at once a most expensive medium and one of the most difficult to handle. Films of dissent often deal with very complex issues. And films of dissent are not likely to get official sponsorship. Thus, the film-maker who somewhat surprisingly uses films to dissent has to fight for the particular cause espoused by his film, and he has to fight also to have his film made and shown.

In the commercial system successful film-makers overcome the ordinary difficulties of film-making. But they never have to struggle to show their films since the film's producer takes that responsibility. In most instances, the subject of the film is lifted from literature or the theatre and is, therefore, readily accepted. Besides, the film establishment knows its audience. It has experience in dealing with particular themes and genres. And that is a great support to the film-maker. Moreover, adherence to this cumulated commercial wisdom ensures patronage.

The maker of a film of dissent, on the other hand, is a loner and too often a loser. His dedication and skill—rhetorical, aesthetic, political, economic and social—are admirable. Yet, even when he has the stamina to produce a potentially useful film, he still has the momentous task of having his film shown to the right people, at the right time and in the right environment, understanding that "right" here often means "left". He can succeed in this only to an extent, rarely warranting the effort that has gone into the making of his film. Thus, unfortunately, too few people see too few films of dissent.

All of this concurs to show that if a film is to be a voice of dissent, then, the very concept of film, its nature, its function, its mode of production and consumption have to be thought over afresh. That is because film as it now exists is part of a system; it is produced and consumed according to the requirements of that system. But that situation must not be allowed to prevail in the case of films of dissent if these films are to play their role in society. To start with, it must be admitted that a film of dissent is not just a film expressing a divergent view, it is or at least should be a different type of film.

A so-called commercial film is produced by one or a few individuals. A dissenting "documentary" film must be produced and consumed by a community in a co-operative mode. If the community is too small to afford the production of a film, then an alternative medium, perhaps a slide show or even an exhibition of photographs, must be sought. On the other hand, rarely would the community be as large as a nation.

The commercial film is produced for efficiency: grossing the largest possible receipts. The co-operative's film is produced for sufficiency. It must be designed by a group for its own use and with its own means. In that situation the film-maker has to play a role very different from his usual directorial role in the commercial set-up. In a co-operative, not only his role, but his method of production, his aesthetics and technical standards are dictated by the needs and capabilities of the group. But at the moment most makers of dissenting films operate exactly as if they were making films for the establishment. That is the flaw.

For, if you anticipate that your film may be put on the national or even on an international network, then you have to use equipment suitable for telecast, you have to meet the technical standards set by the great networks. But these standards are not required by the community nor are they within its means. Hence, if you are interested in making dissenting documentaries, forget about national exposure, about festivals at home or abroad, about national or international awards. You cannot normally disagree with a system and be fully integrated in that system. The system would subvert your film, not your film the system.

Our consciousness and imagination have been so deeply colonised by the ideology of the market that we find it almost impossible to imagine a scenario different from that proposed by that ideology. We think that there is no alternative. We want to change things—because the injustice we witness is unbearable—but what we want to change has penetrated us to such an extent that whatever we do tends to reproduce that which we want to depart from and to change. The co-operative mode of production and consumption is an alternative. Shall we have the courage to explore it? The words of Moses Coady, the great leader of the co-operative movement in Atlantic Canada might inspire us: "if the masses of the people have become, in a sense, slaves, it is because they have not taken the steps or expended the effort necessary to change society." The creation of films in a co-operative mode may be an important step towards changing society.

Institutions sponsoring the making of documentary films should demand that their films be made in a co-operative way. Otherwise, these institutions will reproduce the very mode of production which finally has to be by-passed if people are to create alternative methods of communication. Every new film made is in itself a victory, but the creation of alternative channels of communication is the main goal.

## REFERENCE

Bedford, David and Sidney Pobihyshchy, "Towards a People's Economy: The Co-op Atlantic Experience", in *Interculture*, Vol. xxvi, No. 3, Summer 1993, Issue 120.

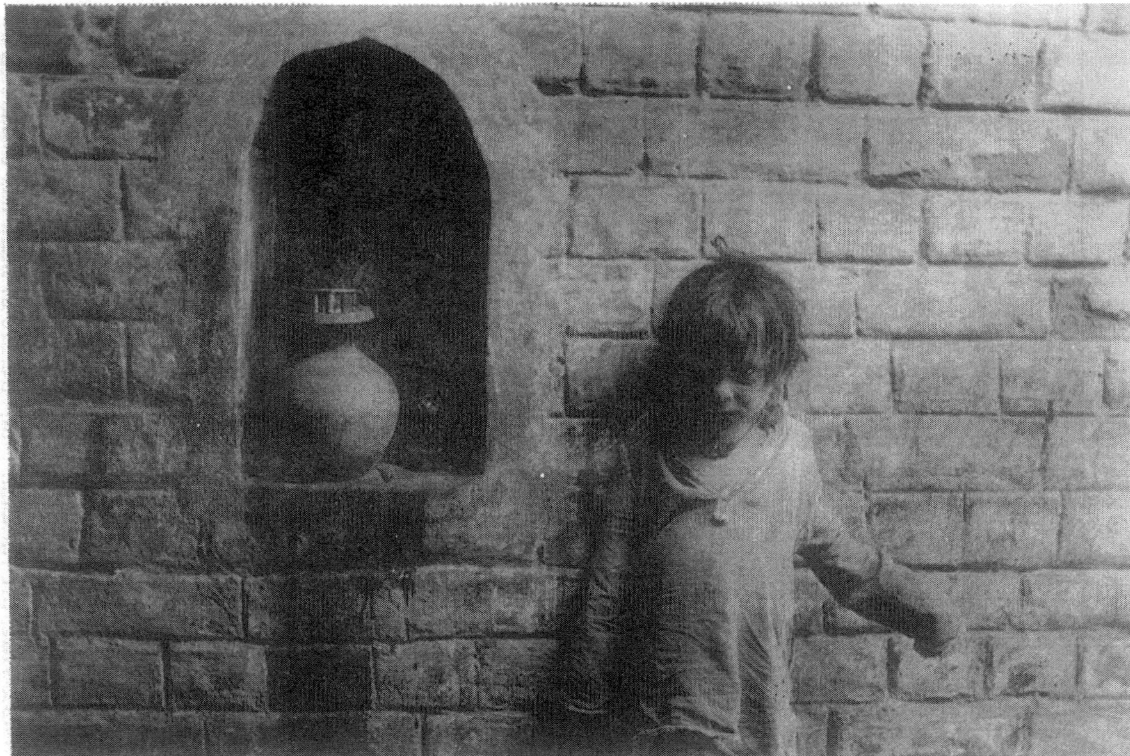

20. Every new film made is in itself a victory, but the creation of alternative channels of communication is the main goal.
Brian Balen

# 29. Film Scholarship

Verbal languages call for two levels of competence, namely, literacy and literature. One who has literacy in a particular language is able to speak, write and read with a minimum of fluency in that language. But a language is not used only for day to day communication. Poets and novelists, for instance, use language, usually writing, to express feelings and ideas worth sharing with other users of their language. What they write constitutes literature. Literature is shared, and it stands the test of time. But while all the people having literacy in a particular language know to use that language, all the people initiated to literature need not be litterateurs, that is, they need not write novels or poems, for instance. They are expected solely to "read" literary works critically.

In the last century or so, a new language has been created: movies. It is a language of moving pictures, quite different from verbal language, like one's mother tongue, for instance. Yet, from the beginning of the cinema there has been a tendency to compare film language with verbal language. The comparison is mostly misleading. Still, it endures. That is why, one can ask, "what are the equivalents of literacy and literature with regard to motion pictures"?

The equivalent of literacy in movies is film appreciation. With this difference: one who has developed a degree of film appreciation, is not expected to make films. The equivalent of literature in films might be called film scholarship: again, a film scholar is not expected to make films, not any more than a student of literature is expected to write novels.

These considerations are very important in the context of the new courses and programmes in cinema studies recently started in Calcutta at Jadavpur University (Department of Film Studies), Calcutta University (Film Study Centre) and Chitrabani (St. Xavier's College, Film Studies Courses). True, the National Film Archive of India has conducted a yearly Film Appreciation Course of 4 to 5 weeks for over twenty years. Film societies too organise occasional study programmes. But the systematic study of film as an academic subject is a new development in India.

The disciplines that lead to film scholarship are collectively designated as "film studies" or "cinema studies". What film studies deal with is rather easy to guess, apart from having a look at any syllabus: the psychology, sociology, history, aesthetics, economics and censorship of films. Add, perhaps, particular subjects like violence in films, the star system, the influence of films on children, etc. What is more interesting, though more difficult to state, is the type of competence which can be expected from a film scholar, more particularly from a student of film studies on completion of his course. To be sure, the student is expected to know something of each of the aspects mentioned above, like sociology, aesthetics, etc. But in addition to these, the student is expected to grasp the implications of films in society.

These implications are many. A few are discussed here. The degree to which the student grasps these implications indicates his level of film scholarship.

*Films arouse emotions.* The student should be aware that all films use particular strategies to engage the viewers and arouse their emotions. She should be able to identify these strategies in at least a few types of films.

*Films convey concepts.* The students should know that attempts have been made to utilise film language to directly convey ideas. S.M. Eisenstein, for instance, claimed that he could film Marx's *Das Capital*. Of course, he never did it. Students should know the potential and the limitations of the film medium for conveying abstract ideas.

*Films are industrial products.* The students should realise that all films are industrial products and they should appreciate the inevitable consequences of that fact.

*Films are texts.* The student should be able to receive any film as a text, that is, as a signifying system to be "read" or "worked upon" by the viewer.

*Films are socio-cultural products.* The students should be able to identify some of the factors that make a film a socio-cultural product and they should understand how these factors work.

*Films articulate ideologies.* The students should be able to discern the influence of the various ideologies, mostly inspired by materialism or idealism, on the making of films and on the discourses occasioned by films.

*Films reformulate myths.* The students should be able to approach certain films as myths generated for the purpose of founding, validating or legitimising particular social formations.

*Films are simulations.* The students should be sensitized to the fact that one aspect of the cinema is the simulation of "reality". They should realise that through that aspect the cinema takes over from earlier modes of spectacles and naturally opens up to experiences of "virtual reality".

*Films are art works.* The students should appreciate the aesthetic qualities of films and should be able to identify those elements that, given cinema's technology, are more specific to the medium of cinema.

A film scholar having acquired some of the competence described earlier would by virtue of that same competence be able to deal with the other media as well. The old distinction between film, television, radio and the press cannot be maintained because all the media are interrelated, broadcast the same discourse, and serve the same interests.

Cinema studies are the royal road to understanding the communication media. And understanding the media fosters the understanding of one's society and of one's place and role within it. Any media can be used as a starting point of media education. But film studies are at the heart of media education, because all people watch movies, all people love movies. However, that very love of the movies can make it difficult for the student to consider films as an object of academic enquiry. Only a rigorous academic discipline can enable him to break the spell of empiricism and accede, if not to a science of film, at least to a scientific approach to films. Film studies start from the film experience of the student, guide her into an appreciation of that experience and give her the concepts enabling her to deal with her experience critically.

However, film studies are the royal road to media education on one important condition: they must open up to the other media, especially those of television and of virtual reality technology. That is why, to indicate the wide scope of film studies, it may be necessary to replace the name "film studies" by expressions like "screen studies" or "image studies", or "media studies". Films would, of course, retain their glamorous aura, but film studies would gain by being stripped of that aura.

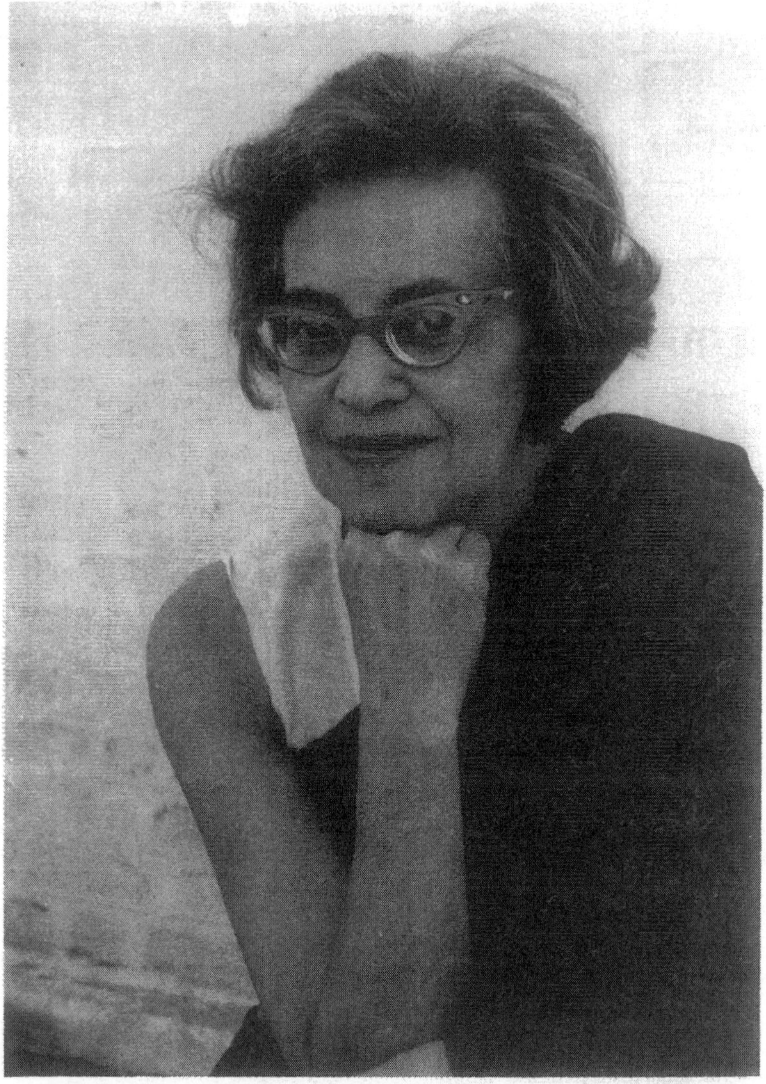

21. Marie Seton (died 17 February 1985), biographer of Sergei M. Eisenstein and of Satyajit Ray, spread film appreciation in India for over two decades (1965-85). This picture was taken when she was lecturing at the Film and Television Institute of India, Pune, during a special course in film appreciation (1967).
Gaston Roberge

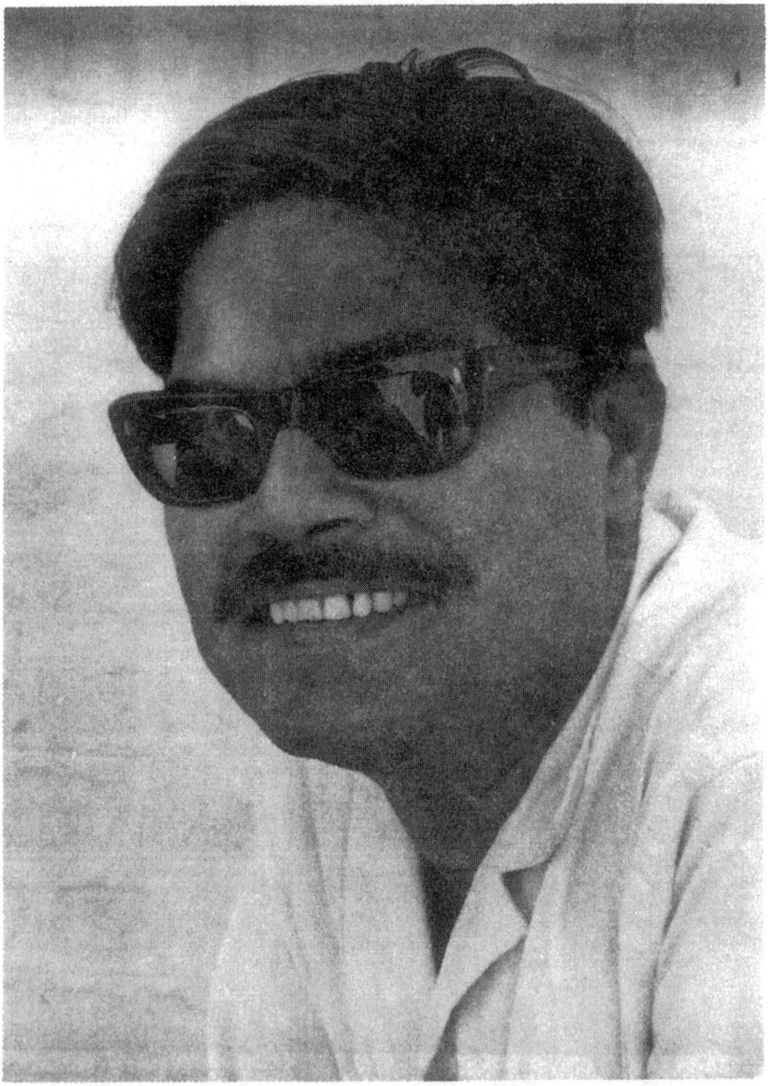

22. Satish Bahadur, the first full-fledged professor of film appreciation in India. He taught the subjcet at the Film and Telivision Institute of India, Pune, since its inception in 1960.
Gaston Roberge

# 30. A Film Industry for West Bengal

West Bengal made a good start in film-making nearly one hundred years ago, when cinema began here and everywhere else all over the world. Within a few years, Bengal was able to produce excellent films which were appreciated locally, of course, but also in some other parts of India. Later the Bengali cinema created stars like Uttam Kumar and Suchitra Sen who ranked amongst the greatest in India. It contributed talented directors, craftsmen and artistes to the Indian film industry. Above all, it enriched world cinema with masterpieces that bear the stamp of a distinguished culture.

And yet, today, the film industry in Bengal is almost dead. Over the years, it has come to be to the all-India film, what the latter is to foreign films, especially the American film. In spite of the tremendous talents available in Bengal, the Bengali film industry is at a disadvantage in its own milieu. It exemplifies the familiar situation of a so-called underdeveloped industry. But in this case, underdevelopment is measured, not so much in relation to foreign countries, as it is to India's own film industry. The Bengali film industry was not born underdeveloped: it sank into underdevelopment. The competition with the all-India film has been unfair. Not because of unfair practices (these are not excluded, of course) but because of the disadvantage of Bengal's smaller industry and audience.

Successive governments in West Bengal have tried to help the local film industry, but the efforts have not given the wanted results. That is, no doubt, because people in Bengal think of cinema in terms of either "trash commercial" or of "art". They want to have nothing to do with "trash commercialism" and they believe that "art", having its aim in itself, cannot be produced for profit. They fail to see that cinema, art or thrash, can be a sound and lucrative business.

Yet, if there is one industry that can thrive in Bengal, it is the film industry. For, every other boy or girl here wants to be a film director, a film-maker or an actor. And the surprising thing is that every other boy and girl probably has the talent to live up to that dream. In fact, for a film industry to thrive, the main requirement, after capital and assured distribution, is, of course, talent. West Bengal is richly endowed with this natural resource. Talent is not an ordinary resource, though: it does not get exhausted when used. The correct utilization of talent generates more talent.

The big production centres clamour for access to free markets which they eventually inundate with their products. But the other production centres, that is, the vast majority, where each one is smaller in size require protection: above all they need stable distribution outlets and an inflow of capital.

It may be that in the past, Bengal has wanted to save its industry mostly for reason of regional pride. But pride, however legitimate, is not enough to ensure success in business. You need mercantile acumen. You need a pragmatic approach to the industrial aspect of film. You have to accept that films, even the greatest film masterpieces, are industrial products. Masterpieces or "thrash", they cannot survive unless they are sound business propositions.

On the other hand, in order to revamp the Bengal film industry more than love of films or "cinephilia" is required. You need a film scholarship that can address the more "trivial" aspects of the cinema: its being a business and its being a popular cultural product. Economics and cultural studies should inform the new discipline.

The fact that Indian films, including Bengali films, are not allowed in Bangladesh and viçe-versa has always eluded my understanding. The restriction seems to be a case of suicidal self-inflicted damage.

With over 70 million inhabitants, West Bengal is nearly as populous as, say, Germany, and much more populated than France. Yet, these particular countries do produce many more films than West Bengal. It is high time Bengal got out of its complacency about belonging to the country that "produces the largest number of films in the world". Yes, we produce nearly 1000 films in a year. But if you look in a yearly book like *Variety International Film Guide* for 1993, you will find that India with her 1000 films gets hardly 5 pages while the USA gets more than 20 pages. So does Canada with its population of hardly 27 million and its few films.

Are we ignored internationally, or do we simply get the meagre attention we deserve? Surprisingly, Toronto is one of the places (apart from South-East Asia) where (in September 1994) Indian films have been greeted most enthusiastically. "Our films", have yet a long way to go before they can compete with "their films" to use the late Satyajit Ray's words . However, it is not competition abroad but development at home that is required (again "Ghare Baire"!). A much more aggressive effort is needed. For instance, I do not see why our Bengali films could not be dubbed at the time of production in Hindi, Tamil and Malayalam for wider distribution in India.

The question facing the film industry, its well wishers, the trade unions, and the government is "what type of help and, above all, what approach, would make the West Bengal film industry prosperous again?" The rest of the country need not worry in this respect. On the contrary, films produced in Bengal and distributed in other parts of India could contribute to enhance the popularity and respectability of the medium. And on the whole business would be the better for it.

However, so many instances of government intervention, have made one thing seem certain. While the government is called upon to help financially and organisationally, it should not take things in hands, but leave them to the private sector. I am persuaded that given sufficient support and incentives, the film industry in West Bengal would rapidly recover. This would have two main spin-off effects: more film-related jobs of the type our youths love, and a prosperous medium in which to assert our identity and counter those cultural elements in foreign media which most of us rightly object to.

## REFRENCE

Guback, Thomas H., "Should a nation have its own film industry?", in *Directions*, Programme on Communication and Development Studies, Northwestern University, Vol. 3 (1989), No. 1.

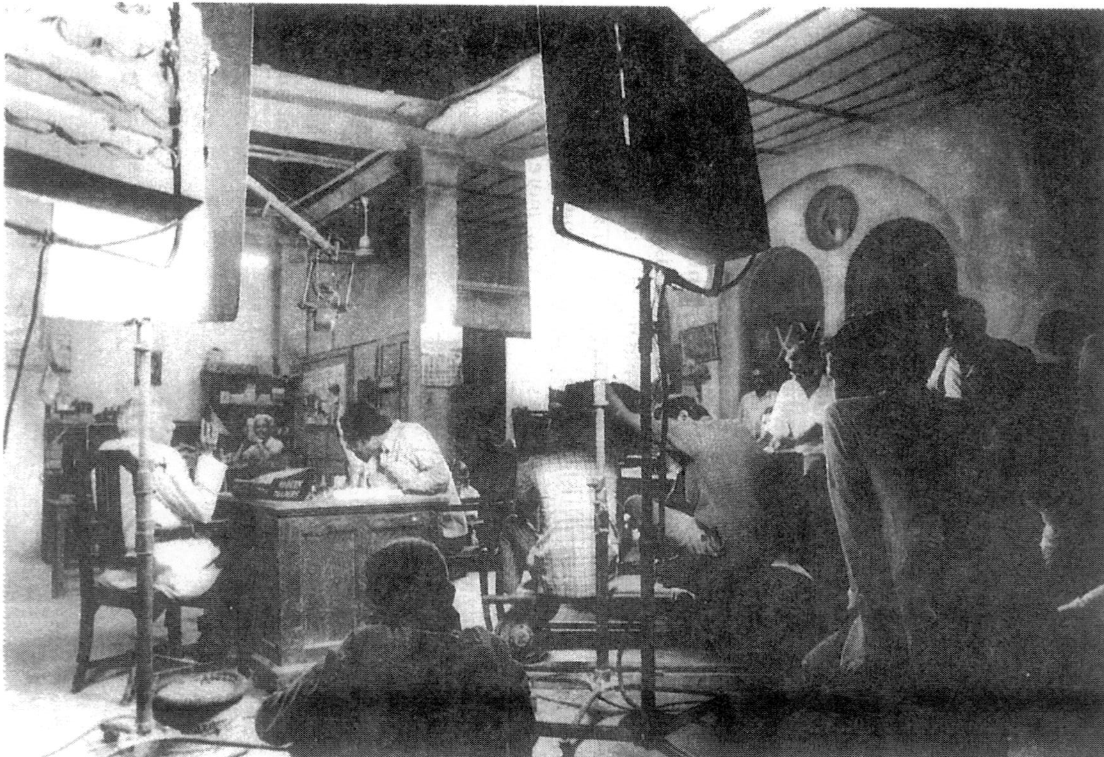

23. It is not competition abroad but development at home that is required. On the sets of Satyajit Ray's *Jana Aranya*.
Brian Balen

# PART FOUR

# CINEMA AND DEVELOPMENT

# 31. *Jesus '71*: A Girl, Little and Mute, has Learnt to Play the Flute ...

Any Bangladeshi film dealing with the 1971 liberation war of Bangladesh would almost of necessity conjure up images of atrocities perpetrated by the then enemy, the Pakistani army. War, after all, never is a gentle encounter. Hence, a film on the 1971 war would be difficult to make because these images of atrocities are too recent to be historicized yet. Memories are too vivid to allow the mind to abstract experience, to rationalize it, and to place it in perspective. The mind cannot, as it were, "handle" the material. Memories flash on the mental screen, in close-ups that remain unconnected and refuse to be organised into a narrative. The function of narrative, precisely, is to work meaning out of disparate events. Through narrative a certain mastery over past events is achieved. But in *Jesus '71* the narrative does not fully master the material, and the film presents a collage of "memories of the war" alternating with pastoral views of Bangladesh. Much of this has documentary touches. But although a work of art always has documentary value it never is just a documentary. However, if *Jesus '71*, achieves the density of art in parts only, it is not just a documentary either. In the midst of the horrors, an image of peace and serenity can be seen emerging: a girl, little and mute, has learnt to play the flute.

*Jesus '71* (*Ekattorer Jishu*, in Bengali) was shot in 16 mm, after a very short story by Shohariyar Kabir, published in 1985 by BRAK, Dhaka, in a booklet of eleven stories for children. The poetry of Kabir which made the story delightful for children is absent from the film, and some scenes of gruesome violence in the film can be objected to as pointless and unnecessary. A few passages of the film's version which I saw in Dhaka on 15 June 1993 are surely unsuitable for exhibition to children. This is somewhat surprising since the story was written for children. But such are the vagaries of film adaptation.

*Jesus '71* is set at the time of the war between erstwhile East Pakistan (now Bangladesh) and West Pakistan. A priest regularly proclaims the Gospel in his church and visits the villagers. The people of his parish flee under the attack of the West Pakistan army. The priest also leaves the place with a group of sisters. Desmond, the sacristan, however, decides to stay on. That humble man has a habit of making crosses. After a brutal attack by the army the sacristan finds a little girl, all alone, and speechless. The sacristan takes her under his protection. But the girl cannot utter a word, not even her name. At a loss, Desmond teaches her to play the flute, a simple instrument made of betel leaves. The girl keeps playing the three notes Desmond taught her. In course of time, a group of youths, a unit of the Liberation Army, take refuge in the sacristan's hut. They conduct a number of successful attacks on the Pakistani army. Finally, they themselves are caught. Desmond denies knowing them, in an all too obvious reference to Peter's denial of Christ. The three youths are crucified in front of the church. Desmond cries in despair. Later on, as he still busies himself making crosses, another group of youths arrives.

The film was directed by Nasir Uddin Yousuff, produced by David Pronab Das, cinematography was by Baby Islam, the music by Shimul Yousuff. The main actors were Pijus Bandhyopadhyaya, Humayoun Faridee and Zahir Uddin Piar.

*Jesus '71* does not fully accede to the condition of art because it is not rigorously informed by a single thought or emotion. The script is the main weakness of the film. Otherwise, the technical aspects, especially the camera work which is often marvellous, are excellent. These include editing, music, sound and visual effects, acting and, of course, direction. In a word, all the elements to make an exceptional film are there. But these elements could not be marshalled in the service of a formative impulse, probably for the reason discussed above, namely, the events alluded to are too recent. The alchemy of memory has not yet transmuted them. Still, in expressing their sense of shock and horror, the film's makers groped for a medium and found it in music, a music played with a folk instrument used by children. If the nameless girl can be taken as a symbol of the newly created nation, the film suggests that art resources are available among the people to create the song of Bangladesh in a mode of peace, joy, harmony and, one hopes, reconciliation. The slogan

"Joy Bangla", however energizing it may be, does not seem to be sufficient.

## I

## A FILM ABOUT DISCOURSE

*Jesus '71* is about discourse. Strikingly, sound and words play an important role in the original story. Four types of discourse are brought in conflict within the film, and accordingly the film itself can be divided into four episodes centred on the characters who utter the discourses.

### I. The Priest

He is a "man of the book". His main task, it seems, is to read the Bible to his church audience, mostly elderly women since the men, presumably are waging the war. The priest's reading of the Passion narrative is intercut with scenes of a man running for his life. The man's speech apparatus can only produce the sounds of a person out of breadth under extreme strain: he utters no words nor can he utter any. The reading of the passion of Christ in this scene appears at worse irrelevant, at best a detached comment on the flight of the running man. The priest has the words, but these words do not relate to "reality". The use of an old translation emphasizes the distance between sacred text and contemporary people and events. The story from which the film is adapted was published in a book whose cover, designed by Rafikun Nabi, shows a man standing in front of three crucified youths and holding a book open—the Bible—as if to read from it. The opposition between written word and action is conveyed.

When the priest is not reading the sacred text in the isolation of his church—the building itself is isolated at the far end of an empty field—he either thinks deeply in the rectory or goes around with a hieratic demeanour, exhorting people to put their trust in God. For the priest, the "Kingdom of God" has little to do with human affairs. His church progressively becomes empty, as the faithful flee under the invasion of the army. There is hardly anyone left for whom the priest can read the Bible. And the priest's role shrinks to insignificance. He then becomes preoccupied with the safety of the sister's serving in his parish. He decides to flee with them. In an atmosphere of liturgy the six or seven of them walk in a line towards the boat—the bark of Peter? the

Church?—which will take them to safety. In spotless white robes, they embark the boat. The "spirit of God" blows their sail away in the distance where the horizon merges with the sky. That is, where the institutional church seems to belong, somewhere between earth and sky. The Church in *Jesus '71* does not claim to be angelical, but yet it would not dirty its white robe. Neither quite heavenly, nor really earthly. Can what is said here of the Church apply, even if with nuances, to all religious establishments of Bangladesh in the early seventies? The "priest", it would seem, must be silenced if religion is to become relevant. But can the sacristan be a substitute for the vanishing priest?

## II. The Sacristan

In sharp contrast with the white robed and manicured priest and sisters, Desmond, the Santal sacristan, is unshaven and dressed somewhat shabbily in black clothes. He is a counter-priest. But he too is a man of the book. He too recites the Bible in season and out of season. When the priest is no more, the sacristan takes over. There is no one in the church. So what? The lip service must go on. The sacristan places hundreds of candles in the church—in the benches, that is, in place of the faithful. And as he lights the candles he utters the words which the priest had left out from his reading: "I have come to bring the sword." This passage of the film is reminiscent of the way Pasolini has made his Jesus recite relentlessly lines from the Bible in his *The Gospel According to Mathew.*

The sacristan would create a new church—if he had people around him. But he, like the priest, is too much a man of the book and too much a man of the institutional Church to be of great help to the youths of the liberation army. He does collaborate with them, though, but under threat he refuses to acknowledge that he "knows" them. When they are crucified he can only cry to God in despair. Actually Desmond is obsessed with the cross. But his is a particular view of the cross of Christ.

## III. The Mute Girl

The girl is a character created by the film's makers; it is not given in the original story by Shohariyar Kabir. Her presence, therefore, is the more significant. It is the sacristan, whom you might call a sinner, in contrast with the righteous priest, who finds her and relates to her. But she cannot speak. She was made speechless by what she saw and heard.

Ordinary language is inadequate to name them, to put them, as it were, into words. Only art and religion can transcend concrete events and order them into an integrated whole. Since words fail, Desmond talks to the girl through music: three notes only. And she responds. I have already discussed this mode of expression.

The moments when the girl plays the flute are amongst the most beautiful and meaningful of the film. There we reach the simplicity and density of art. The little girl, eventually, is killed by the Pakistani soldiers. Her death is pathetic but was it necessary? Should she not have survived?

## IV. The Youths

The youths hardly say anything whenever they appear in the film. Strictly, they have nothing to say because they have everything to do. There is here a situation similar to that which arose at the time of the Bangladeshi film *Beder Meye Josna*. In that film a bad king is reconciled with the poorest of his people. When the discursive mode of the film failed to bring about the desired effect in the political life of 1992, the bad king that is, the then President of Bangladesh, was removed not by discourses but by direct action. The youths of *Jesus '71* are in the active mode. But when they are crucified they are acted upon and they become "words in somebody else's discourse", which is always the situation of the powerless.

Like the little mute girl, the youths have no names, and we hardly ever see their faces. Their anonymity may have its own significance. But the protagonists of an historical event as well as the protagonists of a drama are not people in general, but particular people: they are characters with their own motivation, their own specific responses to people and events. Characterisation is lacking throughout *Jesus '71*. At the end of the film you do not know much about any of the people appearing in the film. They are like symbols only. Desmond, comes closest to "being" someone on the screen. But the narrative gives him too little scope.

Thus, the ritualistic reading by the priest, a reading without any historical moorings, a reading from a book—however sacred it may be—is of no use. Attempts at historicising the sacred text by the sacristan quoting text out of context can only fail. In time of crisis, as the youths demonstrate, there remains only action as a suitable form of expression. Since the priest would not engage in action, he had to be taken out—literally—of the film. But when action is over, the discursive mode—if at all possible—is of little use. The meta-language of art is required.

## II

## THE DISCOURSE OF THE FILM

*Jesus '71* is about discourse, and the discourse is about the cross. *Jesus '71* proposed a metaphor of the cross to sublimate deaths, which, it can be argued, are not and should not be made sublime. They are the pragmatic, concrete, historical response of human beings to actual situations. There is hardly anything sublime in that. Paradoxically, there is some grandiosity in the exit of the priest. But the sublime here is hardly admirable! It smacks of the romantic. Romanticism may have inspired large chapters in the political history of humankind. But a materialist view of history has no place for romanticism.

The film opens with the abstract painting of a cross without the crucified. The cross is blood red, with blood dripping in long red lines on the canvas. This is not a concrete cross of wood and nails, but a painting, thus, a representation of the cross and, indeed, what the film offers is a certain view of the cross. The cross is too red not to allude to, by association, the hammer and the sickle. A disjointed "trimurti" is thus created: the historical, concrete cross of Christ, a representation of the Cross, the hammer and sickle.

After the titles roll on the screen, the film starts with a scene of the sacristan painting clay crosses in black. At the end of the film before the three youths are crucified, the sacristan is making a small cross—again without the crucified. The youth, perhaps, have to occupy the empty place.

The sacristan is obsessed with the graphic symbol of the cross, and so are, it would seem, the makers of the film. Not a few Christians would feel uneasy with the bloody image of the cross offered by the film. They would feel that the cross of Christ is a victorious cross and that the crucified is now a risen Lord. They would feel that the Christian message is mutilated if the cross is detached from the resurrected Christ. They would feel that if human suffering may rightly be compared with and even united to the suffering of Christ, then at the same time the suffering must be illuminated by the resurrection of Christ, and his gift of the Spirit of love, joy and peace. Humankind does not need the cross of Christ unless it is the cross of Christ risen from the dead.

In the novella the idea of the resurrection is clearly brought in by the fact that when the youths come to him, Desmond is reading the chapter in St. Mathew's Gospel on the resurrection of Jesus. In the film the context of Christ's resurrection is not provided. The film suggests that if some youths are killed for the country, other youths will replace them. But will this process go on and on? That thought is hardly comforting.

The resurrection in which Christians believe does not mean simply that Jesus remains with humankind. The main point is that from the Resurrection onward Christ is victorious over sin and death. The believer who shares in his death also shares in his risen life, even now, that is, even before undergoing actual death. In other words, the Resurrection of Christ is as relevant as his death is to human, historical, life.

It is difficult to live at once the reality of both the Cross and the Resurrection. Without the Resurrection the Cross would only be an unbearable burden to humankind. On the other hand, there can be no Resurrection without the Cross. But the cross of humankind is transfigured by the Resurrection of Christ, powerfully and irreversibly.

## Conclusion

As was suggested above, painful experiences like those of the 1971 war require the metalanguage of art or religion to be "processed" and integrated into human life. This process is required, otherwise the experience remains like a festering wound. In *Jesus '71* an attempt has been made to deal with the liberation war in both the poetic and the religious modes. The attempt has been largely successful in both the modes. While the film lacks characterisation and narrative cogency, it nonetheless achieves moments of genuine poetry, notably in the sequence where the mute girl plays the flute. The film is also partly successful in its elaboration of the metaphore of the cross. True, Christian theologians will argue among themselves on the meaning—and thus, the ideal representation—of the cross. But such a discussion is not in the province of film-making. The image of the cross projected by *Jesus '71* is valid and useful, even if it remains open to discussion. It confers meaning and context to the death of the youths of the Liberation Army.

As part of the process to integrate the experience of 1971 the film presents the view that institutional religion—in this case the Catholic Church—was totally absent from the liberation movement: men where fighting for freedom and getting killed while the priest was busy protecting the virtue of the sisters of his parish. Only those who have lived the events of 1971 can say whether this view is correct and, if correct, to what extent it can be generalised.

In all, *Jesus '71* provides a basis for a much needed "memorisation" of the war, and as such can be the occasion of a step towards reconciliation. But, as the long segment of the film on the priest suggests, reconciliation seems to be needed not only with the Pakistani army, but also with institutional religion.

## NOTE

At the end of his essay entitled "Karoyar" in his *Life Remembrances* (*Jeevansmriti*) Rabindranath Tagore has these lines:

> It must be said here that a mind, filled to the brim with a recently experienced event does not necessarily promise a good piece of writing. On the contrary, an abundance of over-emotive sentences unfold. But as a total separation of the thought and the thinker does not work, a complete identification of thought with the thinker fails. The colours of poetry best appear when the paint-brush of memory is applied. Direct perception acts as a constraint and our imagination may not secure the space it owns, unless it, to some extent, breaks out of such controls. The artist should be somewhat detached, not only in the realm of poetry, but also in other creative areas. It is necessary that control should be bestowed to the creator who resides within our heart. If the subject-matter of a composition overwhelms and lords over that creator then the art produced turns out to be a mere reflection, not a representation.
>
> (Translation by Utpal Basu)

Film scholar Siegfried Kracauer has similarly written in an essay on "Photography" (1927):

> As long as they (memory-images) are embedded in the uncontrolled life of the drives they are inhabited by a demonic ambiguity; they are opaque like frosted glass that hardly a ray of light can penetrate. Their transparency increases to the extent that insights thin out the vegetation of the soul and limit the compulsion of nature.
>
> (*Critical Inquiry*, Spring 1993, Vol. 19, No. 3, pp. 421-36. See p. 426).

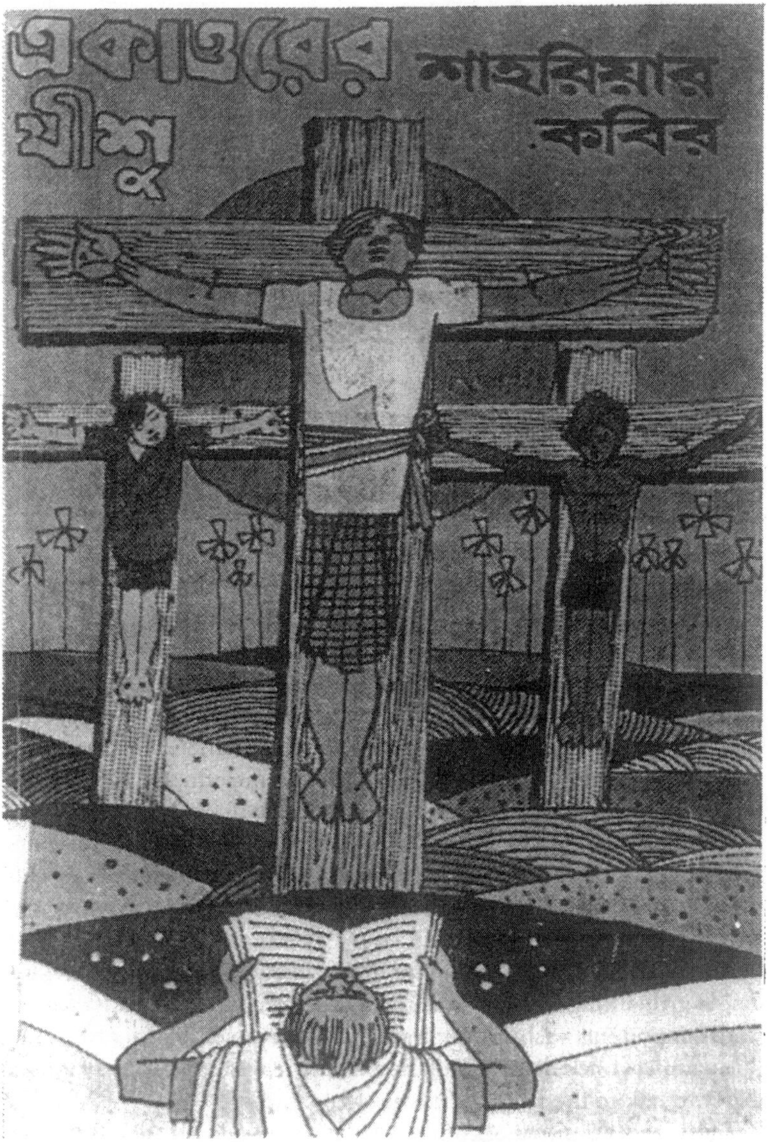


24. The story from which the film is adapted was published in a book whose cover shows a man standing in front of the three crucified youths and holding a book open—the Bible. The opposition between written word and action is conveyed.

# 32. *Beder Meye Josna*: The Girl Who had Three Fathers

I have had the opportunity of seeing the Bangladeshi film *Beder Meye Josna* once, while visiting Dhaka. I enjoyed every moment of this fairy tale. Indeed, I appreciated the film so much that I venture to offer the following thoughts, aware that I do not know sufficiently the social and cultural context, but hoping that my ignorance will permit me to give a candid response to the film.

What struck me first was the un-cinematic quality of the film: but I soon began to enjoy that quality as I discovered that I was in fact watching a performance of folk theatre augmented by the cinema. Then I did not mind the frontality of so many shots, the groups of people standing in the background for the sake of the camera, the theatrical manner of delivering the lines of dialogue, the melodrama. All this was augmented, I say, by the powers of cinema: close-ups of beautiful young lovers, crisp editing, folk songs rendered with the acoustic purity which only cinema makes possible, costumes that belong to another world, impossible fights that can happen only in imagination. All this lifts you up out of the ordinary in a world larger than life. A pleasant escape.

What can be more delightful for the majority of people than to see a simple girl talking straight to a king? *Beder Meye Josna* in addition to escapism presents wish-fulfilling situations: love, sex, and above all the affirmation of one's dignity, and the exciting realisation of one's fearless ability to talk to the rulers of the world.

True, there are moments when the film verges on vulgarity. But then, what is vulgar? The word vulgar comes from a Latin word meaning people. Thus, vulgar means popular. But popular comes from another Latin word which too means people. In fact the Latin had two words for people: the vulgar belonged to the lower social strata, while the popular belonged to the higher classes. So, it seems, the vulgar is what is popular among the lower class people. It's class determined. Like taste. Talking about taste and vulgarity, one indicates one's social and emotional roots.

But all this keeps us at the surface of the film, as it were. What is the story about? Why does it move me so? For I did find the movie "moving". And I wondered why. Could it be only the story? No. Though a fairy tale, the story is too melodramatic, too contrived, in my view, to explain its fascination on my mind and heart. What actually makes me wonder most is the character of Josna, a girl who has three fathers.

First, Josna is the daughter of a man (the wife is no more) who happens to be a judge, the guardian of the law. I see him as representing "dharma", what is perhaps most precious in people's life. The source of stability and security. But Josna has been bitten by a snake and her father cannot do anything to save her. She is like in a sleep. In despair he places her on a little raft and entrusts her to the gentle river, this most pervading presence in Bangladesh, an image of the maternal womb of nature. Attached to the body of little Josna is a note: if you can help this child, please do so. The river carries the "sleeping beauty" with motherly care to the hut of those I can only call "snake-experts", gypsies belonging to the lowest social group. But these simple people know the secrets of life and death: they know how to master snakes, these primal symbols of fertility, life and death. Above all they know how to cure anyone who has been bitten by a snake. Under their care little Josna awakes to the life of a "snake expert". She learns to live and to love. As the tale would have it she comes one day to perform in front of the royal family. And, of course, the Prince falls in love with Josna. But this love is forbidden: Josna does not belong—so the King believes and everyone with him—to a sufficiently high class to be a suitable wife for the Prince. But again the fairy intervenes and the Prince too is bitten by a snake. He is, of course, saved by Josna. But the King would not allow the lovers to marry in spite of having promised to Josna that he would give her whatever she might ask for as a reward for saving the Prince's life. She wishes to marry the Prince who, after all, has loved her first. The King is offended by her request and refuses. The Prince rebels against his father's unjust behaviour. The King sentences him to death. But the Queen Mother intervenes and arranges for both the Prince and Josna to live in exile in a forest. After several episodes, Josna finds her real father in the Judge, the King allows the marriage of his son with her, and he welcomes as his own people the "snake experts" who have saved and brought up Josna.

Note that from the start it is established that Josna belongs to a high class family, indeed to the royal family, since her father is the brother of the Queen Mother. Thus, the taboo separating the social strata is not actually broken. It might have been interesting to create a story in which the Prince marries a girl actually belonging to the social group of the "snake experts". But, I submit, breaking that taboo would have created insecurity in the audience. The audience enjoys the relationship between Josna and the Prince, so long as she is thought to belong to their social strata while not actually belonging to it. But the audience might not have been able to identify with one of theirs falling in love with a Prince. The audience can enjoy that forbidden relationship only if it rests on a misunderstanding. The relationship is wish-fulfilling and does not disturb the social order.

From her real father, the Judge, Josna receives her *dharma*. From the "snake experts", she learns life saving techniques: she acquires a priceless culture. But it is from the King, who actually is her uncle, that she is given her position in society. The King determines her political status. Thus, her fathers introduce her into the realms of religion, culture and politics.

Her father, the Judge (religion) cannot give her the fullness of life and he must entrust her to the river (nature) and to the "snake experts" (culture) who are in close contact with the primal elements: snake, river, blood. This seems to suggest that religion complemented by people's culture makes it possible for one to take position, freely, in the political order.

Thus, when I look at Josna and ask myself, "who is she?" it seems to me that in her eyes I see the thousands of thousands people of Bangladesh. In a word, for me, Josna stands as a symbol of Bangladesh with her three fathers: religious, cultural, political.

Can it be that the large audiences who saw the film have perceived this more or less consciously? Can it be that the audiences have found comfort in the reconciliation of the king with the "snake experts" and through them with the lowest social groups? But that reconciliation occurs only at the level of the story. Josna's story, in fact, functions as a myth. A myth is an attempt to reconcile in the mind the contradictions that are experienced in daily life. Myths have a stabilizing, reassuring function. But there are other stories: the parables. These stories subvert myths and prevent societies from remaining stagnant in the comforting illusion of reconciliation. It remains to be seen whether there can emerge an artist who, rooted in the same cultural soil, would create the "parable" capable of subverting the myth of Josna. It remains to be seen whether the audiences who have found comfort in the myth of Josna would accept to be called upon to take a more realistic position, even if it must be one of contradiction, in the real, historical political order.

I saw the film and wrote this review in early May 1990. Little did I know that within six months the people of Bangladesh, in an action-parable, would remove the then President of Bangladesh, Mr Ershad. The "bad king" would not get reconciled with the poorest of his people. He was removed.

The film *Beder Meye Josna* demonstrates that popular films deal with the social reality of the masses who see them. These films may propose unrealistic solutions to social evils and to that extent they may be said to be escapist, but as such popular films are fantasies dealing with the existential problems experienced by the audience. That is why such films are a good basis for group discussions.

The Bangladeshi Josna film was remade in West Bengal and released under the same title. The West Bengal version, though quite different from the original one, proved very popular too. No doubt, the people of West Bengal had heard of the success of *Beder Meye Josna* in Bangladesh and they wanted to see the version made available to them. But the social situation in West Bengal is different from that prevailing in Bangladesh, and, accordingly, the film elicits a different reading.

Chitrabani, a communication centre based in Calcutta interviewed forty-five West Bengal people who had seen the West Bengal version of the film. The interviews suggest that (a) several viewers made a "political" reading of the film saying that "our leaders too do not fulfil their promises", an allusion to the fact that in the film the king does not keep the promise made to Josna. Moreover, (b) women were struck by the positive role played by a woman in the film. One of the women interviewed said, "even though the character (Tara) was a woman she could play an important role". It is interesting that in the film that young woman had to disguise herself into a man, with moustache and pants, in order to play her role.

# 33. *City of Joy*: Fantasy of a Wounded Psyche

This essay deals with the film *City of Joy*, not with Dominique Lapierre's book *The City of Joy*. In departing significantly from the book it is supposed to be based on, the film can give an impression to the viewer who has not read the book that the latter is as bad as the film. This would be unfair. In spite of the ethnocentrism and the developmentalist ideology of the book, I had welcome it as a useful fiction which could draw the attention of millions of people to the real living conditions of slum-dwellers in Calcutta and elsewhere. Unfortunately, Ronald Joffe's *City of Joy* has hardly anything to do with either Dominique Lapierre's fiction or the reality of the Pilkhana slum, still less the reality of Calcutta.

The dream-like sequence opening the film *City of Joy* suggests that the film deals with the psyche of its protagonist, Dr. Max. Played by Patrick Swayze, American "par excellence" with his hyper-vitality, Max suffers from paternal disapproval and from a sense of failure because a child died in his hands on the operation table. How Dr. Max lands in the dispensary of the "City of Joy" is part of the nightmare. One might dismiss it as poor screenplay, but the nightmare is a mechanism whereby the American persona, itself an illusion, is delineated against the fiction of some other people who can be called collectively "The Other".

What are the characteristics of that Other, as seen in the Joffe's film, as he appears in the film and whom Dr. Max encounters as the fictitious background image of himself? Firstly, the Other is lascivious. Indeed, as soon as Dr. Max settles in his hotel room in Calcutta, he is seduced by a young girl who is thrust upon him as a matter of routine. In fact, the girl works for some antisocials who beat up Max and rob him. The lasciviousness of the Other is associated with violence.

The second characteristic of the Other is that of a rapist. For what does the son of the "godfather" do to Hasari Pal's daughter in the abject enlarging of her mouth with a razor blade if not rape her symbolically or physically? It is Dr. Max, of course, who is seen repairing the damage and suturing the girl's mouth.

A third characteristic of the Other is that he lives in a society where no change can take place without outside intervention. Indeed, the misfortune of the slum-dwellers is seen as resulting solely from the action of local people on the milieu. Outside pressures seem to be inexistent in the creation and perpetuation of slum life. Moreover, the police is shown disparagingly and the government is hardly mentioned. There seems to be no one, except for a nurse and Dr. Max, both American, to care or to dare to do anything to bring about change. The American is the interventionist.

Fourthly, the victims are innocent, naive, helpless, childish creatures, not unlike the diminutive people whom "the Phantom", in the comic strip of that name, rescues always single-handedly, and always violently. Hear them: they do not speak American English. How could the Other master that language? But they do not speak Indian English either. This would make them sound too mature and too educated. See them act: they behave as they are assumed to behave by outsiders. Calcutta slum-dwellers could discover through the film new ways to have fun with a rickshaw or new ways to behave during the first rain of the monsoon. Only an outsider could imagine them behave as they do in the film.

In Lapierre's book the Indians think like Frenchmen, in the film they are seen to act like Americans. Hollywood has appropriated an Indian locale to project the American persona. The image of a Calcutta slum had to be adjusted to the pre-conceived ideas of the film's makers about slum-dwellers and their presumed reaction to an American presence.

Thus, the Other is a mixture of bad and good. We have seen that Other time and again in the American media. The "bad" Other, like Sadam Hussein, must be aggressed. And the "good" Other, like the poor(!) Kuwaitis, must be saved from the oppression of the bad Other. Intervention is a moral imperative. This is the domestic ideology which the American media grotesquely project worldwide to justify countless American imperialist interventions. In *City of Joy*, it is American Max who first revolts against the social order dictated by the local "godfather". He succeeds in drawing the slum-dwellers in the revolt. In the process these people suffer immensely. And docile rickshaw puller, Hasari Pal, grows into a potential killer. His own children have to plead with him so that he does not eliminate the godfather's son. The Indian man has "developed" into the image of his American mentor.

The image of the Other as a rapist is an Amercan domestic commodity In the Gulf war, for instance, the actual or alleged rapes perpetrated by the (bad) Iraqis convinced many Americans that Bush's war was just and necessary. The war, they came to believe, was not determined primarily by American interests. The scuds of Sadam Hussein, like immense phalluses, were countered by antimissiles that were, of course, "patriots". Sex associated with nationalism.

It is clear that the characteristics mentioned above are not at all the necessary characteristics of slum-dwellers. They are, however, necessary fictions to establish the American persona. Without the bad Other and its correlated good Other, the American could not see himself as the saviour of the world. And he needs to see himself as a saviour in order to police and aggress those who threaten his interests.

After the failure of Vietnam, the American psyche is wounded: Uncle Sam is displeased. The Gulf war, the greatest show on earth, was meant to nurse the wound and to boost the morale of the American people. It was successful to a large extent, but it seems that the Vietnam wound requires yet more stitches to heal. *City of Joy*, whatever the noble or not so noble intentions of its makers, adds a few stitches. But these won't hold because the film is so bad.

A viewer has nicknamed this film "City of Horror". Indeed, *City of Joy* offers solely a voyeuristic montage of tableaux of horror. It is indeed a horrible film which makes Calcutta appear a place of horror. As for the idea of making a replica of a slum just to make a film, it too is horrible. The point was, to paraphrase an oft quoted saying, not to show the slum, but to change it.

If there is any joy in *City of Joy*, it is the joy of the American doctor. For he finds a motherly woman whom he can love and who helps him regain his lost confidence in himself as a doctor. As for the Indian hero, Hasari Pal, he bravely dies out of the film: his daughter is getting married. Yet, his exit, like the rest of the fim, is a show.

In an article on "Sexuality in the Gulf War", from which this essay draws, A. Farmanfarmaian points out that at the time of the 1893 World Fair, there appeared a cartoon showing Uncle Sam leading the nations in a joyful dance. The song attributed to Uncle Sam was:

It's done! It's done! The show and fun
We've had for six months past;

I have made the world stare
At my wonderful fair...

to which the nations sang in chorus:

For he's a jolly good fellow...

It was necessary, if horrible, to build the obscene set of the slum in order that the show might go on. To whomever got the idea all will sing:

For he's a horrible fellow...

## REFERENCES

Farmanfarmaian, Abouali, "Sexuality in the Gulf War: Did you measure up?", in *Genders*, No. 13, Spring 1992, pp. 1-29.

Roberge, Gaston, *The Ways of Film Studies, Film Theory and the Interpretation of Films, with an essay on Freud by Dr. Somnath Zutshi*, New Delhi: Ajanta Publications, 1992. See pp. 210-19 for an analysis of Dominique Lapierre's novel *The City of Joy* (1985).

# 34. *Ganashatru*: Straight from the Heart

I saw *Ganashatru* at a very private show and I liked it immensely. It's nothing like any other Ray film, but it is a Ray-film all right. I would describe it as a gem. It has the compactness of a finely wrought gem. The form is so perfect that the anecdote seems to be a mere pretext for the form itself. Yet, the anecdote is well dealt with. And form here does not mean formalism, that is, form for its own sake. It is as if the form of the story is the form of something else, and that something else is so much more important. One senses that the story is not the main point of the film. The form raises the film to an abstract level where it becomes—not a message or still less a thesis—but a cry of hope and joy... beyond the "story". And this point is reached through a series of infinitesimally small increments downward, until it bounces upward in well measured leaps.

The film is like music, although I am not familiar enough with musical forms to say which form it is. Music is never the sound of something. It is the form of an emotion. So also this film, as I see it. The extraordinary thing is that the form of the film is also, of course, the form of a story which is told in a very arresting manner. But it is not polemical. It just is.

The acting is, of course, an important element of the form of the film. Each character gives a superb performance. Saumitra is the ever *Ganabandhu* (the public friend). But Dhritiman is the perfect counterfoil with an amazingly mature performance. The film being based on a play, it is normal that it be an "actor's film", but this means it is above all a "director's film", since acting in film, perhaps more than on the stage, has to be "directed".

*Ganashatru* was certified for exhibition on 4 April 1989. I wrote the previous paragraphs on the film in a letter to a friend, dated 19 April 1989. Subsequently, I was appalled at the bad reviews the film elicited in Calcutta. Bad not because they did not praise the film, but because they were so wrong in their approach. Of course, a film made after a play by Ibsen invites comparison between film and play. But it should soon be evident that such a comparison in this case is a blind alley simply because Satyajit Ray was not interested in the play as a play. In a word, Ray was not interested in Ibsen. He just took the story of the play as a pre-text for his own film text.

The second misleading avenue explored by critics was whether Ray was taking a stance against Hindu fundamentalism. Ray has never shown any sympathy for religious fundamentalism. But he never was a pamphleteer. However much disturbed he may have been by the increasing manifestations of religious bigotry and fanaticism at the time of the making of *Ganashatru* he had other personal preoccupations. The question of religious fundamentalism is more than just a background to the film, but, on the other hand, the film is not prompted, as it were, by that question. *Ganashatru* cannot be said to be a film about religious fundamentalism. Always having his audience in mind, Ray provides good stories. He found a good story in Ibsen's play and he adapted it for his audience. In the very process he expressed his own childlike joy at being alive, at being able to make a film, at being supported by his family.

Ray had been very ill and he had been forced to inaction for almost five years. At last he could again make a film, even though his doctor had set stringent limits on his shooting schedule. Would he then attempt to "film Ibsen" as others "stage Ibsen"? Or would he then raise his voice against fundamentalism? Anyone watching the film carefully, without "a priori" ideas on what the film is supposed to be, would answer no, emphatically, to the two questions.

The film opens with an image of a stethoscope on a table with a telephone in the background. The camera moves slightly in the direction of the telephone,,pauses for a moment, just as a hand begins to dial a number. Then, the camera pans further along the cord linking the telephone to its receiver in the hand of Dr. Gupta, the protagonist of the film.

It is not irrelevant to remember that Ray had suffered from heart attacks and that the film was his first "communication" after a long convalescence. Do I overstretch the "line" from stethoscope to telephone if I say that this film is "straight from the heart". Indeed the whole film is a personal communication of Ray. What about? Communication, creativity and youthfulness. That takes us far from Ibsen and from Hindu fundamentalism.

Dr. Gupta has something to say. Something vital for the people under his care. Namely, he knows for sure that the elixir distributed by the local temple is polluted and poisonous. However, vested interest would not let him have his say. He wants to write in a newspaper. He is not permitted to do so. He attempts to talk in public. His meeting is disrupted and he is silenced. Stones are thrown at his domicile. His daughter loses her job. He loses his. He is told to leave the place. But as Dr. Gupta is about to sink in despair his daughter, her friend and local students take up the fight. No, all is not lost. One can still live. One can still communicate, one can still be creative. What a joy! *Ganashatru* is Ray's hymn to life, to creativity, to joy.

I had the good fortune of discussing all this with Satyajit Ray himself. As I was telling him of the form of the film, using my hand to trace in the air a curve going up, then down and up again, he interrupted me and he said something like, "yes, it goes up in three steps" and with his hand made a gesture upward in three steps.

This triple ascending movement works well in music. But as a dramatic denouement it may be found a little abrupt. Up to that point in the film the dramatic form and the potential musical form blended harmoniously. Here, perhaps, the musical form—freer than the dramatic form—has escaped, as it were, on its own. Whether the drama ends too abruptly in *Ganashatru* is open to discussion. But those who are insensitive to the musical form which the drama supports will not appreciate the graceful exhaltation of the film's ending.

I said that the opening image with the stethoscope and phone suggests that the film comes straight from its maker's heart. There is another possible meaning explored by French critic Charles Tesson. The stethoscope can be seen as an extension of the camera. Through this film Ray listens to the heart of the world, and invites the spectator to both see and listen. In fact, perhaps more than in his previous films, off scene sounds are heard as part of the diegesis of the film. That is especially true of the shouting outside Dr. Gupta's home: first the mob's shouting and then the students hailing Dr. Gupta as a hero. Indeed, Dr. Gupta's home is a stethoscope. The home is listening to the world—(Ghare Baire!).

## REFERENCES

Tesson, Charles: "Le bruit du monde" in Cahiers du Cinéma, No. 422, July-August 1989, pp. 20-5.

Ray has given us an indoor film entirely turned outward, towards the mad energy of the world. *Ganashatru* is hard cut and hard cutting, dry and sharp like silex. *Ganashatru* is a very great political film, the most profound and unbiased look at all that agitates the end of this century: the return of religious fundamentalism, (the religious faith belonging to the people and because of that, sacred, out of reach), its collusion with politics (power, the institutions and control of the masses), the economic (its touristic exploitation) and the mediatic (rumour and heretical defamation). p. 22

About the final sequence when the students come in support of Dr. Gupta:

that collusion of politics and poetics (the students have been mobilised by a students' theatrical troup. G.R.) in a same voice is really a miracle, and it is beautiful that people whose life is committed to art, to representation, in the end occupy the field of politics. (p. 24)

Fisher, William, "Entretien avec Satyajit Ray", in *Cahiers du Cinéma*, No. 417, March 1989 (an interview of Satyajit Ray during the filming of *Ganashatru*). Ray said:

I never believed and I still do not believe that a film can change society. In Soviet Russia, for instance, the revolution had already taken place (when Eisenstein made his films. G.R.). p. 61

During the major part of my life I was an unbeliever. But there are certain things which I can't explain, and which science too cannot explain. ... As one grows older, when death approaches, I guess one begins to be a believer. But I still do not believe in rituals.

I totally identify with Dr. Gupta, an honest man who does not fear the truth. I understand his motivations, his sufferings and his joy at the end. I fully agree with what he says. I believe in the supremacy of science. (p. 60)

# 35. *Shakha Proshakha*: The Heartbeat of Time

Who will save us? Who will heal our wounded humanity? How shall we regain sanity and, above all, peace? These are the questions *Shakha Proshakha* raises with compassion, yet urgency. Time passes on. Irretrievably. No answer is imposed. However, elements of answers are offered. When the branches are detached from the tree, they can do nothing. Estranged from their father, the Prabirs of the world will gamble life away and the Probodhs will cheat. Each of them will consider himself a success. Only those who stay in vital communion with the tree can acknowledge their mediocrity: they are saved by humility.

Since *Ganashatru*, the films of Satyajit Ray are more than ever before, direct statements emanating from a man who has undergone deep experiences. Not only are these later films informed by the experience Mr. Ray had of illness, but they vibrate with the thoughts that preoccupy him more forcefully after that illness. *Ganashatru*, was concerned with environment and fundamentalism of all sorts, but it was first of all a hymn to life and to creativity. After recovering from a heart attack Ray was again able to communicate, to create. Perhaps none of his previous films had been so deeply personal. *Shakha Proshakha* features a seventy year old man who, at the peak of his fame, has a heart attack and recovers. But he recovers to what? To the discovery of corruption around him. Moral turpitude, a sort of illness from which, it would seem, one cannot recover.

All of Satyajit Ray's films are very personal. But previously it was the creative impulse that found its expression in films of relevance. Now, in his seventies, Ray is seized with the urge to express his thoughts. His means of expression or language being "film", the appropriate film form emerges to convey these thoughts.

One could argue, as indeed Ray himself has done in an interview, that long ago, when he was hardly forty-five, he had imagined the story of Ananda Majumdar. And hence the personal aspect of *Shakha Proshakha* should not be exaggerated. True. On the other hand, it is now that Ray made that film. And am I wrong in finding in elderly Ananda (Ajit Bandopadhyay) a facial resemblance with Ray? Be this as it may, the critic has to be clear as to what he wishes to achieve: a biography of the film-maker through a scrutiny of his films or a "reading" of his films against the background of the director's private life and in the context of contemporary social life. The two, personal experience and films, cannot be separated. But ever since film criticism has taken a semiological orientation, critics have preferred to see films in themselves. They seek to "read" meaning in films in the context of the social discourse of which films are a part. Whether or not a particular meaning was intended by the creator of a film is a matter that pertains to his biography, not to film criticism as such. The fact is, a film-maker is always greater than his film, because no artwork can fully encompass the personality of its creator. On the other hand, the significance of a film is always greater than whatever a film-maker has wanted it to be, because significance is infinite. However, the test of the validity of a reading is whether it can be communicated and shared. A viewer may not read a film the way a critic does but the viewer can come to see the sense inherent in the critic's reading. Even film-maker Jean Renoir said that he learnt about his films from critic André Bazin.

*Ganashatru* dealt with the external environment. *Shakha Proshakha* deals with the internal environment of the men and women of our time. The film examines the human values that make life worth living and without which there is no peace, whether in society or in each one's heart. These values are lost or enhanced according to the type of relationships men and women entertain not only with so-called "nature" but also among themselves, and especially in relation to women.

When I said earlier that Ray seems more concerned with saying things than with creating forms, however relevant, I certainly did not mean that the present films are not well crafted. I mean that the primary impulse seems to be different. Form flows as if effortlessly in the service of thought. In *Shakha Proshakha* once the stage is set, as it were, the film takes off and proceeds, in marvellous film terms. Ray, at his best, describes the Majumdar's relationships vividly and subtly. There are open conversations at table, there are more intimate conversations in the sleeping rooms. Each couple's relationship and each person's relationship with the others are directly projected. What immediately appears is the estrangement of all. The four sons are estranged from each other and two of them from their wives to the extent that they are estranged from their father. Proshanto who seems completely alienated is, in fact, in deep communion with each and all of them. At the beginning he wonders whether his brothers should not have come to celebrate their father's birthday? He is also acutely aware of what is happening to his father: he will be sick, but he will recover, he feels. And at the end of the film, when Dingo innocently discloses to his grandfather that corruption has crept into the family, Proshanto immediately foresees the devastating effect of that disclosure on his father and he comes to comfort him.

I cannot help seeing this film as an illustration of the words of Christ: "I am the true vine, you are the branches. Whoever remains in me, with me in him, bears fruit in plenty; for cut off from me you can do nothing" (John 15, verse 5). Let nobody misunderstand me. I am not saying that Satyajit Ray has wanted to make a commentary of this scriptural verse. I just say that I read the film against the background of that verse and, as a result, the film is the more meaningful to me.

In a corrupt world, one way of maintaining one's integrity is to take refuge in the purity of music. But one cannot hope to take refuge in music and still live in this turbulent world. Such a solution would only lead to complete detachment, and, therefore,to a form of madness. Proshanto illustrates this tendency lived to its ultimate consequence. This renders him unfit for work, the ultimate value of Ananda's Victorian universe. Probodh feels that Proshanto should be sent to a mental hospital. But Pratap too, in the eyes of both Probodh and Prabir, has done something "mad" in leaving his job because he found corruption there. Even Ananda is not exempt from failure. If we are to believe Pratap, in years past, Ananda was more preoccupied with "work" than with love for his sons. In a way, Ananda too was "mad": work was music to him. He is not the trunk of the tree, but only a main branch.

By the end of the film it is evident that sanity lies in neither work as worship nor honesty as a rule of life, but in love. Probodh does not love. At the end of the film, when he takes leave of his father and puts his hand in that of the ailing man he does not communicate love: and he leaves his father sad as never before. But when Proshanto places his hand in that of his father on the latter's chest, he communicates love and a profound peace. When one loves, one is at peace with the world and with oneself.

Often during the film Proshanto is seen listening to music, of Bach, we are told. At one point, when Pratap and Dr. De discuss the case of Proshanto, the latter is listening the Gregorian chant of "Kyrie Eleison" (Lord have mercy). I am thankful to Ray for having refrained from making of his film a "musical". We have just enough music to sense the atmosphere of joy and peace in which Proshanto takes refuge. At the end of the film, the Bach music lingers in our minds until, perhaps, it fades into the "Kyrie Eleison". For, indeed, who will save us? Who will heal our wounded humanity?

# 36. *Agantuk*: The Cave of the Heart

*I find myself trying, through my films, to trace the underlying pattern that binds this life together.*

SATYAJIT RAY[1]

*The pattern that connects.*

GREGORY BATESON

Satyajit Ray's last film, *Agantuk*, is one of the six features for which he wrote original stories. It is perhaps the film in which he expresses himself most openly. It is the film that deals with the largest subject, namely, contemporary civilisation. Above all, *Agantuk* is a summative film in which Ray has wanted as it were, to complete a number of projects. I can hope, therefore, to touch upon only some of the aspects of the film, well aware that there are other important aspects which, I trust, other writers will discuss.

## "*AGANTUK*" AND THE "*ALIEN*"

In an interview he had with him, Andrew Robinson had asked Ray if there was any relationship between *Ganashatru* and *The Alien*, the film Ray had planned to make in the mid-sixties. Robinson saw some common elements, like the temple, the journalist, the nexus between religion and money, the Bajoria character. Ray's answer: "It hadn't occurred to me at all.... But now you mention it I can see the point."[2] I am sure Ray would see the point if I were to ask him like Robinson: "Would I be right in saying you've put some of *The Alien* in *Agantuk*?" Manomohan Mitra does not come on earth from a distant planet, but he sees the world from the point of view of an outsider, which is what he has become as a result of living among so-called primitive people. Like the Alien, Mitra is benevolent. For, Ray has made this his last filmed character[3] not altogether an Alien, but a stranger, a new comer, and even a loving "uncle". After all, the name "Manomohan Mitra" means the "lovely friend". The "agantuk" is closer to people than the Alien. For although Mitra left his immediate family thirty-five years ago, he has always remained with people, in search of what makes them human.

## PROBING INTO CONTEMPORARY CIVILIZATION

Like the Alien, Mitra is able, so it seems, to read other people's thoughts. Above all, like the Alien, he has eyes to see. To see through, to see into, to see large in other words, to probe into contemporary civilization.

Probing is for Ray the fundamental task of the artist. In 1957, writing about the making of *Pather Panchali* he stated what was and remained his objective:

> to observe and probe, to catch the revealing details, the telling gestures, the particular turns of speech.... The more you probed the more was revealed, and familiarity bred not contempt but love, understanding, tolerance.[4]

All the Ray films have been probes into "reality", they all lead to understanding, tolerance and love. This is true especially of *Agantuk*. Ray had given the Alien special eyes to probe into the world around him. He gave Manomohan powers of perception that come from a long experience of observing people of cultures different from one's own, especially simple people like children or like tribals. Coming back to Calcutta after a long absence Manomohan can share the results of his probing into contemporary civilisation. The probing is ruthless: (a) the damaging effect of money (a theme explored in *Kanchenjunga*, *Nayak*, *The Alien* , etc.), (b) the stupidity of war (*Goopy Gyne Bagha Byne*), (c) the true meaning of civilisation, (d) various aspects of Bengali culture, like food, hospitality, music, "adda" (e) the faith in each other which makes love possible and human life worth living, (f) and above all the wonderful complexity of the world.

## THE UNDERLYING PATTERN THAT BINDS THIS LIFE TOGETHER

In *Agantuk* "the underlying pattern that binds this life together" (Ray) or "the pattern that connects", (Gregory Bateson) is shown to be a common experience of life. Anila (the niece) recognizes that Manomohan is her uncle when the latter sings to her a song of her childhood.

Conversely, the uncle recognizes Anila as his true niece when she responds to the tribal dance and joins in. The identity provided by family blood relationships and established by documents like a passport is not at all sufficient. What binds this life together and, finally, what binds people together, is the common experience they have of life. There may be a touch of romanticism in Ray's setting the recognition by Mitra of the humanness of his niece in the surroundings of Shantiniketan, among tribals. Ray, after all, is a city man. And he is well aware of this. This awareness has made *Pather Panchali* possible. The curiosity and wonder of Durga and Apu at the train and the telegraph wires is the reverse of Ray's own wonder in front of village life. However, Ray does not suggest that everyone has to actually go to a village. What he does affirm is that a certain "wanderlust" (to use a German word—used in English, we are told!), a "depaysement" (to use a French world, not used in English, I say) a going out of one's own mental universe, a certain disorientation, a freedom from one's artificial moorings, are required.

## RAY'S LIFE PROJECT: TO BE A FILM-MAKER

I said that in *Agantuk* Ray has completed several projects. His main life project was, of course, to be a film-maker. He enunciated this project lucidly in 1948 in an article entitled, significantly, "What is wrong with Indian films?" An article which comes six years before François Truffaut's belligerent and generally wrong headed piece, "A certain tendency of the French cinema". When Ray wrote, "What's wrong with Indian Films?" he was hardly 27 years old, he had not yet made any film, he had not yet met Jean Renoir in Calcutta. His article can be seen in retrospect as the "manifesto" on which is based his entire film work and which he never betrayed. It was not just one of those youthful statements which greater reflection prompts one to forget and for which one can be forgiven. Ray formulated his programme against the background of Indian films at the time. He wrote:

(what is needed) is not more gloss, but more imagination, more integrity and a more intelligent appreciation of the limitation of the medium.[5]

Above all "a drastic simplification of style and content" will be needed. This will be achieved if the film-maker "keeps his eyes open and his ears." For "the raw material of the cinema is life itself".[6]

In an article of 1951, he had also written

For a popular medium, the first kind of inspiration should derive from life and have its roots in it. No amount of technical polish can make up for artificiality of theme and dishonesty of treatment. *The Indian film-maker must turn to life, to reality.*[7]

In *Agantuk* Ray resolutely turned to life, to the reality he could see around him. Earlier on he had explored the theme of an eventual film, *The Alien*. That film was never made. *Agantuk* is a reflection on the same theme, but at a more profound level. *The Alien* would have been fun with wisdom as a bonus. *Agantuk* is much fun too, but wisdom is the main ingredient. One might say that in certain respects *Agantuk* is to *The Alien* what *Ghare Baire* is to *Charulata*. But the last two films are Tagore's, the first two were Ray's own conceptions.

## THE RETURN OF THE HERO

A thematic approach to the film can be complemented by a morphologic approach on the lines proposed by Vladimir Propp in his *Morphology of the Folktale* (1927). As some critics have noted already, *Agantuk* reveals itself to be a tale dealing with "the return of the hero". This pattern of story usually implies that the hero has to undergo certain tests. So does Manomohan Mitra in *Agantuk*. Perhaps was it befitting that a film advocating a return to the source of humanness be expressed in a basic story form that is perhaps universal. But a reflection on these lines, however interesting, should not obscure the fact that the APU trilogy too involves a "return of the hero" after many a test. Apu, indeed, comes back to Nischindipur, his natal village with his child, Kajol. Apu surely sees the village in a new way, for he has matured. Mitra comes to Calcutta, but his return is to Shantiniketan. This is a return of Ray as well. But strikingly, Mitra does not go to Tagore's school of art. He goes to a Santali village. Ray must have been aware of the numerous implications of Mitra's return to Shantiniketan. From an autobiographical point of view, Ray sides with Mitra. For, in spite of his fine teachers at Shantiniketan, Ray discovered Indian art in contemplating frescoes at Ajanta. Similarly, Mitra who too was an art student discovered the source of what Tagore called "the human heritage" in the bison of Altamira. Another implication of Mitra's going to Shantiniketan but not to Tagore's school is that, bypassing Tagore as a secondary source, Ray goes to a primary source, the Santali village. Ray had hesitated to join Tagore's school. He felt himself to be too much of a city man. It is as if he said in *Agantuk*, "if I must go out of Calcutta to Shantiniketan, I may as well go straight to a tribal village".

## WHY A BISON?

Is it not striking that Mitra, the Indian, should be so deeply impressed by a drawing of a bison? Of course, the bison of Altamira is an extraordinary depiction of a living animal. But Ray could surely have used another masterpiece with a similar effect. Why a bison? And what can the bison's connotations be? Historians of religions tell us that there are at least two sorts of deities, those in the sky, labelled ouranian, and those on or in the earth, the chtonian ones. The bison, is biologically related to the cow. The cow is an earthly animal protected by a chtonian god, Shrikrishna. The latter is associated with the aboriginal (Latin "ab origine" means from the origin) people as contrasted to the invaders and colonizers, who worshipped an ouranian deity, Indra. The bison, in a word, has pre-Aryan connotations. The return to the sources suggested by Ray is indeed radical.

## THE THRESHOLD OF MYSTERY

There is a sequence in *Agantuk* which is as important as it is gratuitous. Gratuitous because it does not seem to do much to advance the action, perhaps not even to reveal Manomohan Mitra's character. It is the scene when Mitra has gone out on the Maidan with Satyaki and his young friends. The scene is important because it reveals a concern of Ray: the mystery, the wonder it evokes. Cinema had helped Ray to discover, as he put it already in 1963, that

> although you have roots here—in Bengal, in India—you are at the same time part of a large plan, a universal pattern. This uniqueness and this universality and the co-existence of the two, is what I mainly try to convey through my films.[8]

Sitting on the Maidan Mitra explains to his captivated audience the phenomenon of eclipses. It takes a good two and a half minutes of film time to lead the children to the point where they realize that they cannot explain a complete lunar eclipse. And they are told emphatically that nobody can explain the occurrence. Mitra calls this "magic", in a language that children can grasp. But he is himself fascinated. He exclaims: "I am telling you, of all the wonders of the world, this is the greatest. The sun and the moon, the king of the day and the queen of the night, the shadow of our planet on the moon, and the three heavenly bodies are like three discs of the same size!" Even if you call this magic, I am not sure it will hold the attention of children for a long time. The subject is somewhat austere. It is as if Ray needed an opportunity to express his own sense of wonder. A sense that has grown over the years and led him to the threshold of mystery and of transcendence. Ray, who might be described as an agnostic, had nonetheless an open mind. He was struck by the complexity of things, like the human body, or of events, like the lunar eclipse. These, it seems, cannot occur by accident. In fact, whether you explain it by positing a transcendental force or by admitting the possibility of an immanent accident, there is room for wonder. For, the chances of such accidents happening are almost nil. And yet they occur. In his interview of November 1988 with Andrew Robinson, while speaking about his coming film *Ganashatru* and the belief of the masses in the power of "holy water", he said:

Doctors generally in my experience believe in God, for instance. They pray. My own doctor, my house-physician, says that if you inspect the human body—the incredible complexity of it—you have to believe in a superior force. It can't just happen by accident.[9]

## RAY, CONTINUATOR OF TAGORE

Ray did for Bengali cinema what Tagore had done for Bengali literature. Ray felt akin to Tagore in many ways. This is nowhere shown as strongly as when Ray made his documentary film *Rabindranath Tagore* (1961), a tribute to the great poet, philosopher and educationist. The opening lines of Ray's film applies to Ray himself with prophetic accuracy thirty years ahead of time:

On 7th August 1941, in the city of Calcutta, a man died. His mortal remains perished (on the funeral pyre, GR) but he left behind him a heritage which no fire could consume. It is a heritage of words and music and poetry, of ideas and of ideals. And it has the power to move us, to inspire us, today and in the days to come. We who owe him so much salute his memory.

Over the years, Ray had assumed a unique role in Bengali social life by his cultural impact, by his personal, deep emotional, links with Tagore, and by his fine adaptations of Tagore's literary works onto the screen. He had earned the right not only to translate Tagore into film terms but to interpret him in terms of his own sensitivity. At the end of *Rabindranath Tagore*, Ray had quoted the ending lines of Tagore's magistral lecture, 'Crisis in Civilization' (1941).

I had at one time believed that the springs of civilization would issue out of the heart of Europe. but today when I am about to leave the world that faith has deserted me. I look around and see the crumbling ruins of a proud civilization strewn like a vast heap of futility. And yet, I shall not commit the grievous sin of losing faith in man. I shall look forward to a new dawn, to a new chapter of history when the holocaust will end, and the air will be rendered clean by a spirit of service and sacrifice. Perhaps the dawn will come from this horizon, from the East, where the sun rises. On that day, the unvanquished man retraces his past of conquest, surmounting all barriers, to win back his last human heritage.

These lines read well as lines by Tagore. But one cannot imagine Ray uttering as his own the second part of the quotation, from "Perhaps the dawn will come from this horizon ..." till the end. There is here a sentimental turn, an eccentric flight into the poetic which, I am sure, Ray could not make his. Yet, in spite of this, *Agantuk* has always been to me Ray's equivalent of Tagore's 'Crisis in Civilization'. When he is "about to leave the world" faith in civilization issuing from the heart of Europe, if he ever held it, has deserted Ray. Faith in the present civilization itself, as he sees it, with its corruption, with its diversion away from the sources of life, has deserted him. Like Tagore, Ray does not lose faith in man. But for him man is not an abstract, universal, man, seen in the future. The repository of Ray's faith are the men, the women and the youths of today. In *Agantuk*, it is a present day woman who can sway to the rhythm of a tribal dance. Ray is concerned, above all, with interpersonal relationships and with concrete people's response to life. He goes much further than Tagore. For Ray, it is not enough to see that light is not forthcoming from the West, it is not enough to turn to the East (which Ray himself has done when he discovered Indian arts in a contemplation of the frescoes of Ajanta). For Ray it is necessary to ascend to the very source of humanity, of humanness, symbolised by the bison fresco of Altamira. What matters to Ray is the quality of the perception a human person has of life. The Altamira fresco proves that so-called pre-historic man was more and better sensitive to life than contemporary men and women. Yet, the hero of *Agantuk* and, in him, Satyajit Ray do not despair. In *Ganashatru* Dr. Ashoke Gupta discovers that he can have faith in the youth. Manomohan Mitra discovers that he can have faith in his niece. Humanness in her has not completely dried out. There is still hope.

## THE QUALITY OF "*AGANTUK*" AS A FILM

In this discussion of *Agantuk* I have said nothing about the quality of the film as a film. What about the dramaturgy, that is, about the organisation of the actions? The crisp dialogue? The music? There is no doubt much to say about these. But I am so taken up by the film's significance that I find little interest in commenting about its formal qualities beyond what I said about its narrative structure. Of course, the significance of the film cannot be dissociated from its form. One does not stand without the other. *Ganashatru* may have had the five part structure of a drama, yet that film was informed by a musical structure. The dance towards the end of *Agantuk* and the idea of rhythm it conveys suggest that *Agantuk* is informed by a rhythmic impulse rather than a melodic line. The introductory sequence may at first appear literary with Anila reading a letter. But, in fact, around the immaterial object of a piece of news, Anila and her husband display in a series of alternations a wide variety of reactions which reveal their characters. Enters the bison, and a whole set of characters in a series of *pas-de-deux* and *pas-de-trois* define themselves with regard to it—that is, with regard to Mitra. They perform in the main rooms of a "civilised" house, the drawing, sleeping and dining rooms. What they are forced to reveal is their reaction to the unknown, to life, to the mystery, to others and to self. Dhritiman Chatterjee who had played the counterpart of Dr. Gupta (Soumitra Chatterjee) in *Ganashatru* again superbly plays the counterpart of Manomohan Mitra (Utpal Dutt).

Since I have related *Agantuk* to Tagore's 'Crisis in Civilization', I may as well relate Ray himself to Tagore. Tagore was eighty at the time of his last lecture, Ray was seventy-one at the time of his last film. Both spoke in their elected medium with the authority given by prestige, with the experience given by a life dedicated to art and communication. Both spoke from the unique position of persons "about to leave the world", when one puts one's whole being in what one is saying and one has no time for what is not essential. I have heard a few people claiming that *Agantuk* is not as perfect as were some of the earlier Ray films and, as such, it cannot be taken so seriously. Such a response to *Agantuk* appears to me obtuse, nay, incomprehensible. These same people have told me that a film must be judged by film standards. But, precisely, one of the standards that Ray has established for cinema (and in this he was of one mind with his mentor of earlier years, Jean Renoir) is that it should communicate with the audience. And *Agantuk* does communicate. But one must open one's eyes, and ears. *Agantuk* is a statement—shall I say a testament? Ray did not write it as Tagore did. He has painted it on the white canvas of the cinema, wrestling with time and illness to complete the work. Do you not see that Utpal Dutt gives a human face to the bison of Altamira? That Mitra's character has the impetuous strength of the charging bison? That it has its simple lines, its economy? That it results from a "drastic simplification of style and content"—which Ray had written in his 1948 manifesto the Indian cinema needed? In *Agantuk* is revealed a "pattern that connects", an "underlying pattern that binds this life together". The greatest tribute one can pay to Satyajit Ray in front of *Agantuk* is to see the Altamira bison, issuing from the cave of the human heart and vibrant on the screen.

## RAY'S FAITH IN HIS SPECTATORS

Ray, like Renoir has placed his faith in the spectator of his films. In his second article on cinema, in 1949, Ray quotes Renoir who, speaking about the coming of the sound film, had said:

> It was as if someone had opened a secret door of communication between the film-maker and his audience. It was a great feeling. Everything we did the audience understood. The French cinema could not have made those enormous strides towards maturity without this wonderfully perceptive audience. They helped us all along the way, and I for one feel grateful to them.[10]

## NOTES AND REFERENCES

1. From the commentary written and spoken by Satyajit Ray for B. D. Garga's two-reeler film, *Creative Artists of India: Satyajit Ray* (1963). Quoted in *Montage*, No. 5/6, July 1966. See "Why I make films."
2. Robinson, Andrew, *Satyajit Ray: The Inner Eye*, London: Andre Deutsh Ltd, 1989, p. 344.
3. There is yet another Ray character in screenplay form, made into a film by Sandip Ray.
4. Ray, Satyajit, *Our Films, Their Films*, Orient Longman, 1976, pp. 33-4.
5. Ibid., p. 22.
6. Ibid., p. 24.
7. Ibid., p. 127. Emphasis mine.
8. Ibid., p. 116.
9. Robinson, ibid., p. 343.
10. See note 1.

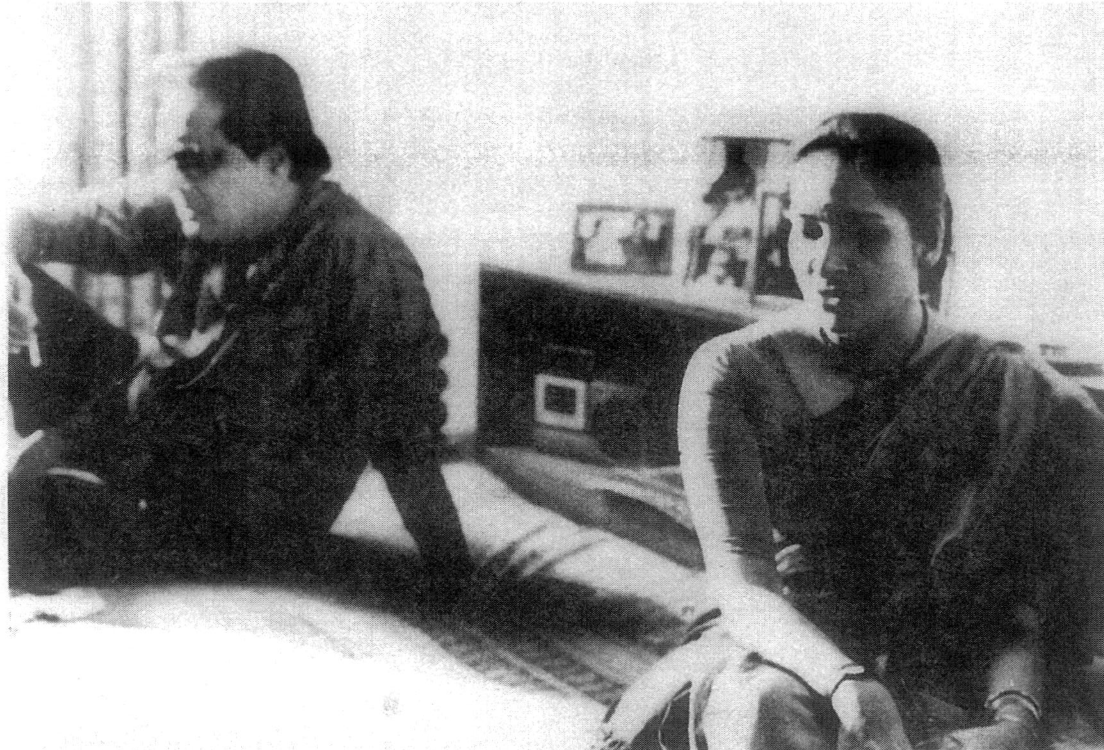

25. "*. . . to observe and probe, to catch the revealing details, the telling gestures, the particular turns of speech . . . the more you probed the more was revealed, and familiarity bred not contempt but love, understanding, tolerance*". Satyajit Ray, in an article of 1957.
Courtesy: Sandip Ray

PART FIVE

# CINEMA AND TELEVISION

# 37. Indian Cinema meets Television: A Close Encounter of a Strange Kind

Television took a few timid steps on Indian soil in 1961. Now, from the sky it is making a full scale invasion of the country. Both indigenous and foreign televisions shall soon be present on the entire subcontinent.

In that context of television's expansion we celebrate the centenary of cinema. Two questions arise: what is the relationship between cinema and television? and what is the future of cinema in the television era? I leave the latter question to prophets. I deal with the former. Namely, how do the two media relate with each other?

## 1. WHICH CINEMA? WHICH TELEVISION?

In the mid-1950s film scholar André Bazin discussed the nature of cinema in the collection of his writings, entitled, precisely, *What is Cinema?*[1] But he was not the first to ask. Before him, already in 1917, psychologist Hugo Münsterberg, a colleague of William James at Harvard University, had studied the psychology and the aesthetics of the new art. His little book had the name then used for cinema, *The Photoplay*. After Münsterberg and Bazin, a good number of scholars have written on cinema. We have something to start from.

In contrast to cinema, television is more difficult to define. In his day Münsterberg wrote "cinema is only 16 years old ...". Cinema may now be a hundred years old, but for most of us in India, television is hardly five, ten, fifteen years old at most. We have not yet come to grip with cinema, how can we hope to deal adequately with television? Moreover, we have not yet experienced the various forms that television can take.

Still, we must begin to consider television seriously: our present response to television largely determines what we shall be a few years from now.

When I asked, "what is cinema?" and "what is television?", I spoke as if both cinema and television were monoliths. In fact, there are many cinemas and many televisions. And that makes it the more difficult to discuss the relationship between the two media.[2]

Surely, all cinema films cannot be lumped together. Watching a silent film of the 1920s, say, *The Battleship Potemkin*, is not quite the same experience as watching *Roja*, for instance. Again, the documentary *Nanook of the North*, does not offer the same experience as science fiction film *Jurassic Park*. Yet, these four films are cinema. And it is possible to enunciate the characteristics these films share as cinema even as we acknowledge the differences between the four of them.

It is not that easy to locate the characteristics of television. That is because much of what we now see on the Indian television actually is cinema tailored to the small screen (most serials are cinema, at times bad cinema). Another chunk of television can be termed illustrated radio (many a news bulletin). But with television ads we begin to experience another language. And interactive television[3] exemplifies yet one more of the forms television can take.

However, in my opinion, it is the musical programme, emteevee, that illustrates what much of television is likely to be in future. I am not speaking here of the television recording of musical performances, however beautiful these may be. I am not thinking of film songs either. I am referring to the musical items that are prepared especially for television with a lot of electronically prepared visuals. These musical programmes are quite popular and they are quite typical of television too. It is not surprising that the teevee musical should be most characteristic of television. After all, the musical was the film genre par excellence during the haydays of Hollywood. In the following discussion it is that type of programmes that I shall take as representative of "television". And, for obvious reasons, by "cinema" I shall mean the ordinary feature film, the story telling film.

As a recording technology, television can be used of course, for any purpose: you can record a drama, whether it be an art work in a theatre, or a real life incident on the street, like the assassination of the late U.S. President, John F. Kennedy. You can record talks, and the teevee viewer knows how many talks while time away on television. You can record sports too. Thus, the television screen, like the cinema screen, provides a variety of experiences, calling for various types of sensibility. And there is no authority to dictate what television ought to be. I shall argue later on this paper that as a television form, emteevee is not accidental at all. It is fully determined.

Even if the diversity of film and television forms is kept in mind, the relationship of television and cinema can usefully be seen as a development of the relationship of cinema itself with theatre. Though, there is more difference between cinema and television than there is between theatre and cinema.

## 2. THEATRE CINEMA

The first people making films soon realised that the new technology could not only record natural events, it could also record pre-arranged events. It could, in a word, simulate and represent human actions. It could tell stories coherently and arrestingly. Cinema was then perceived as a means of spreading theatre. Thanks to the recording capabilities of the cinematograph, it would be possible to make the best plays available to masses of people. Those who cared for social equity rejoiced, and hailed cinema as an eventual democratisation of the theatre.

There were yet two other basic reasons for the interest of film-makers in theatre. Early films were of short duration, 10 to 20 minutes. In order to supply films to the mushrooming theatres stories were needed. And plays, with tested stories, offered a good repertoire. Stories were also taken from the novel. That is because the work of a film-maker is greatly simplified if he has a story to start with. Closer to us in time, even the late Satyajit Ray was always on the look out for good stories. When you produce a film almost every year as he did you need stories. When you produce a film almost every week as the early film-makers did you need stories galore.

Of course, in time, writers began to write directly for the screen. The idea that you can write on the screen with your camera came in the 1950s and 60s with Alexandre Astruc. He spoke of a "camera-stylo". Satyajit Ray whom I just mentioned eventually created stories which he wrote in screenplay form directly for some of his films.

The other reason why theatre and cinema interacted from the beginning of the new art is that cinema is both a mass entertainment and an art form. It always craves respectability. As early as in 1900 French stage actress Sarah Bernhardt appeared in a film version of *Hamlet*. She was subsequently invited in Hollywood. There the film company

Famous Artists in Famous Plays was formed (to become Paramount Pictures in 1916). In the late twenties Hollywood created its Academy of Motion Pictures Arts and Sciences which gives the stamp of respectability to movies at the same time as it sets standards.

Since the 1900 *Hamlet* countless plays have been made into films with various degrees of success. But in addition to straight adaptations of plays there was in the 1940s a school of thought which favoured the making of cinematographic plays. For that school of thought, cinema was but a development of the theatre. As a self conscious movement, cine-theatre was short-lived but it produced some masterpieces, those of Marcel Pagnol (between 1931 and 1940), notably. Yet, as a tendency, the theatrical approach to film-making endures. Even as supremely cinematic a film as *Charulata* bears heavy theatrical marks. And you can see theatre at work in many a serial on the Indian television.[4]

The early enthusiasm of film-makers for theatre, however, was short-lived. It soon became evident that both cinema and theatre had completely different characteristics. Cinema could indeed be used to record plays. But left to its own, cinema tended to come alive and to leave theatre behind. Cinema did not need theatre to create its own presentations. On the other hand, theatre could not be transmitted satisfactorily through cinematographic recording. Without the presence of the actors, recorded stage plays lacked life and appeal.

However, apart from these relationships of convenience between cinema and theatre, there have been fruitful exchanges at the aesthetic level. It can be said safely that all the masterpieces of the theatre have been made into films. Thus, in addition to stories, cinema gained characters and dramatic developments which it was able to absorb into its own aesthetics.

Today, we see television do to cinema what cinema did to theatre. But before we discuss television, we shall consider closely the psychology of the film experience. That will serve as a propaedeutic to television itself.

## 3. THEATRE CINEMA TELEVISION

Münsterberg was perhaps the first to describe with precision the differences between the two art forms of cinema and theatre. He did it from the point of view of the psychology of film. Unfortunately, for reasons which have to do with intolerance and suspicion,[5] his *The Photoplay*, was ignored until the early 1970s. Unfortunately, I say, because it is from the point of view of psychology that the difference between cinema and theatre as well as the difference between cinema and television can best be understood. The history of film scholarship would surely have been different had Münsterberg's contribution been retained earlier. Even a thorough scholar like Jean Mitry did not know of Münsterberg when in 1963-5 he published his monumental *Esthétique et Psychologie du Cinema*, a book which still awaits English translation. But what is more striking is that when Mitry came to know of *The Photoplay*, he dismissed it as "subtle psychological analysis" to which he gave little scientific value.[6]

Almost at the same time as Münsterberg wrote *The Photoplay*, Lev Kuleshov in Soviet Russia conducted experiments which involved the psychological response of the spectator. But Western film scholars did not pay much attention to these "interesting" experiments. In fact, scholars in the West have always shown more interest in the somewhat elusive psychoanalysis of both films and film-makers than in more down to earth psychology.

Sergei Michaelovich Eisenstein, who was well acquainted with the work of Kuleshov, felt that a film ought to correspond to the processes of the mind. He firmly believed that once those processes were known and a method to reproduce them developed, it would be possible to "plough deep in the spectator's psyche" in a specific class orientation, and to produce with precision pre-determined effects.

It should not be taken for granted that because cinema espouses the processes of the mind, a film can be immediately understood by a person who has never seen films before. A case in point is that of the close-up. Indeed, a cinematic close-up reproduces the mental process of attention, when an object grows out of proportion and occupies the field of attention. Nevertheless, at first, spectators were taken aback by CUs. Cinema espouses the processes of the mind, but nature doesn't. Thus, even if the film presentation is naturalistic, it clearly departs from nature and is more akin to mind work than to natural appearances.

I emphasize that point because many of us in front of "television" are still like those movie spectators who saw close ups for the first time. We have to realise that television too espouses mind processes, but not those processes that have so far been privileged by cinema.

Introducing Münsterberg's *The Photoplay* in 1970, Richard Griffith wrote:

> Münsterberg's book is a primer ... we will do well to keep by us as we confront the theoretical adjustments and advances required by mixed media, and the new attack on the sensorium represented by the experiments of Expo '67. This

attack, if that's the word, seems to require a major shift in the attention of the spectator—a new way of combining sense-impressions in the mind—a new imaginative act. (pp. xiii-xiv)

Since Expo '67 the "attack on the sensorium" has not relented, and we are confronted today by television with a new demand to produce "a new imaginative act". Münsterberg's discussion of the psychology of the film from four points of view, namely, depth and movement, attention, memory and imagination, and emotions, is as relevant as ever.

## Depth and Movement

The screen, we know very well, has no depth. Yet, while watching a film we constantly have the impression that the protagonists move towards us or away from us. Looking at the cinema screen is a bit like looking at a mirror. The surface of the mirror too is flat. But if I stand three feet away from a mirror, I see my image three feet behind the mirror, as it were, that is, six feet away from where I stand. The image of myself which I see six feet away is a virtual image. It is as if I saw it through the mirror.

When I watch a film I see, or I think that I see, a virtual image. But it is not my own reflection. It is an image "programmed" by the film's maker. I am not there, but everything invites me to be or feel that I am in the image, though I do not see myself as I do in front of a mirror. I see the film image as if through the screen. The image is created in such a way that I must see it that way. But the film image can be and, at times, has been created so as to produce other effects. Obviously, speaking of "cinema" here I refer to the usual story telling film.

On the other hand, by means of the stage, the footlights, and the "mise-en-scène" arranged in front of me and for me, theatre holds me back, so to say, on my seat. I am not tempted to climb on the stage. While cinema pulls me into its presentation, theatre keeps me out and comes to me.

Television neither comes to me nor takes me in. It just is. It has no depth. It is all surface, and it is indifferent to my participation, indifferent even to my very presence. The teevee image pulsates in isolation. Theatre is unthinkable without an audience at the very moment of the representation. Cinema too requires an audience, though it can be at different times and places. But television is always there. Like the electric power supply, teevee is available whether or not you plug yourself into it. Again, it is like an individual airconditioner which one adjusts for one's comfort. Except that here you have a "mind conditioner".

The scene of the theatre is a cube so concentrated that it implodes upon itself, as it were. The scene of the cinema has no off-scene: it explodes in space. Bazin, who always made use of illuminating comparisons, wrote this about space in theatre and cinema:

> In contrast to the stage the space of the screen is centrifugal—there are no wings to the screen. It is because that infinity which the theatre demands cannot be spatial that its area can be none other than the human soul. Enclosed in this space the actor is at the focus of a two-fold concave mirror. From the auditorium and from the decor there converge on him the dim lights of conscious human beings and of the footlights themselves. But the fire with which he burns is at once that of his inner passion and of the focal point at which he stands. He lights up in each member of his audience an accomplice flame. Like the ocean in a sea shell the dramatic infinities of the human heart moan and beat between the enclosing walls of the theatrical sphere. This is why this dramaturgy is in its essence human. Man is at once its cause and its object.[7]

But television is something else. The scene of television has no depth, it seems to have no finite dimensions—vertical or horizontal, and it bears no relationship with the space around it. It itself is space.

Physical movement on the theatre stage is real. In the cinema screen movement is not real any more than depth. A dot on the screen is seen in different locations, it does not actually move from one location to another one. That, is, it never occupies the intermediary positions which the impression of movement implies.

> We find that the movement too is perceived but that the eye does not receive the impressions of true movement. It is only a suggestion of movement, and the idea of motion is to a high degree the product of our own reaction. Depth and movement alike come to us in the moving picture world, not as hard facts but as a mixture of fact and symbol. They are present, and yet they are not in the things. We invest the impression with them. (p. 30)

In theatre and cinema the movement of objects and protagonists is usually purposeful and directed by familiar laws. The direction and speed of the movement is predictable or at least plausible. But on the music TV screen everything seems to move at random and at various speeds. What will happen next cannot be predicted. Nor does the movement ever come to rest. The television screen presents us with an electronic Brownian motion.

### ATTENTION

The close-up (to which one might add the zoom-in movement), as I mentioned above, reproduces the act of attention.

> It is as if that outer world were woven into our mind and were shaped not through its own laws but by the acts of our attention. (p. 39)

The "as if" must be emphasized, because in the process of "closing up" nothing actually happens to the "real" world. Here, the danger of confusing real world and diegetic world (that is, the world of the film) is not always overcome. Like when Münsterberg writes: "The events without have become obedient to the demands of our consciousness" (p. 38).

Television does not demand attention. Just a floating awareness of what's happening on the screen. As noted earlier television is indifferent to you, and, it seems, you are expected to be indifferent to it.

### MEMORY AND IMAGINATION

Münsterberg felt that

> the photoplay obeys the laws of the mind rather than those of the outer world.

Notwithstanding the fact that most film images are naturalistic,

> In the one (CU.) we recognize the mental act of attending, in the other (Flash Back) we must recognize the mental act of remembering. In both cases the act which in the ordinary theater would go on in our mind alone is here in the photography projected into the pictures themselves. It is as if reality has lost its own continuous connection and become shaped by the demands of our soul. (p. 41)

Of course, the film neither "obey" nor disobey the laws of the mind. It is created by the film-maker according to some of the processes of the mind. That is why after a little training we make sense of images which at first might appear disconnected and incoherent.

If an apple falls from a tree, I know that it will crash on the ground. But my mind can choose to see things differently. What if I imagine that the apple stops falling mid-way and remains stationery in the air? It is easy to represent that in film. Thus, if in a film I see an apple stopping halfway in its fall, I am made to imagine that it is stopping because the film-maker has created pictures and arranged them in the very manner in which the mind works. Thus, when I watch a film, some of my mind processes are directed by the film itself. Of course, no film can ever mimic and, in doing so, programme the totality of my mind. It is clear, however, that cinema and theatre "programme" the mind in very different ways. And television does it in yet another way.

Theatre can allude to facts, but it is very poorly equipped to represent imaginative acts the way cinema does with close-ups, flash backs or flash forwards, and parallel montage, for instance. What mind processes are objectified in musical television where there is no depth, random movement (Brownian-motion like), and no causality, at least in the common sense? The mind processes represented by television are those of the subconscious: associations, condensations, metaphores, metonymies, and others in a seamless and ceaseless flow. These representations, we can rest assured, have their own validity. We have to ask, what principle or agency directs them? and to what end?

### Emotions

These are the emotions which the protagonists transmit to our own soul, and our own emotions with which we respond to the film.

Anthropologist Edgar Morin spoke of identification and projection to refer to these two mechanisms of emotional participation.[8]

Concluding his discussion of the film's psychology Münsterberg wrote:

> The photoplay tells us the human story by overcoming the forms of outer world, namely, space, time, and causality, and by adjusting the events to the forms of the inner world, namely, attention, memory, imagination, and emotion. (p. 74)

American film actress Louise Brooks had understood the same thing when she said:

> The great art of films does not consist in descriptive movements of face and body, but in movements of thought and soul transmitted in a kind of intense isolation.[9]

However, it is not the photoplay that "overcomes the forms of outer world" and "adjusts the events to the forms of the inner world". The agent is the film-maker. The tendency to give the medium the power of an agent is characteristic of a whole school of thought which can be labelled, somewhat imprecisely, "idealist".

But idealism has its charms, as Münsterberg's following lines so beautifully exemplify:

The massive outer world has lost its weight, it has been freed from space, time, and causality, and it has been clothed in the forms of our own consciousness. The mind has triumphed over matter and the pictures roll on with the ease of musical tones. It is *a superb enjoyment* [emphasis mine] which no other art can furnish us. (p. 95)

Beautiful thought, yes, but nonsense nonetheless. For, "the massive outer world has lost" nothing of its weight.

Nearly fifty years after Münsterberg, Jean Mitry too described the experience of watching a film from a psychological point of view. He tried to define what most characterises the film experience. But, a man of his time, Mitry discussed at length the relationship of the film image with what it is the image of, a question which occupied film theoreticians well up into the 1960s, that is, up to Mitry.

The materialist felt that if the link was severed, the image would be more objective. On the other hand, the idealist claimed that the link image-reality should not be broken as it offers the onlooker a view more alike reality itself.

For television, that old debate is irrelevant. Television offers a virtual image without any referent. It does not matter whether the image is or is not the image of something else. For, there is nothing else. The teevee image is pure image. It is what Plato had already called a "simulacrum", a pure appearance. And the appearance (of nothing) moves wildly in a space that is nowhere and offers no place for you to inhabit it.

## 4. THE PLEASURES OF TELEVISION

Frederic Jameson[10] has propounded the thesis that capital has undergone three major internal revolutions. In the 1860s you had market capitalism, in the 1890s you had monopoly capitalism and from the 1940s you have multinational capitalism. These three moments of capitalism used three types of technologies based on steam, electricity and nuclear power. They also had three cultural logics, namely, realism, modernism and post-modernism.

Extrapolating on that thesis Vivian Sobchack[11] proposed that the three moments of capitalism had their forms and institutions of visual and aural representations: photography, cinema and television.

Since we in India have not yet caught up—if that is a correct way of looking at "development"—with the era of multinational capitalism, we cannot hope to fully understand the phenomenon of television, let alone to create an indigenous, mature, television. For, each technological revolution has brought about a "radical perceptual revolution within the culture and the subject". (Sobchack, p. 89) Jameson affirmed that the "prodigious expansion of capital into hitherto uncommodified areas" was paralleled by "a new and historically original penetration and colonization of Nature and the Unconscious" (Sobchack, p. 99).

We may gain an insight into the perceptual revolution under way in India if we revert to the pleasures we derive from cinema and from television, respectively.

"A superb enjoyment" wrote Münsterberg about cinema. And he was right. But he was thinking of aesthetic enjoyment, that is, of the pleasure that form with apt content can give. Although he was fascinated by the psychology of the film, he did not seem to have paid much attention to the psychology of "enjoyment". For, whether or not it achieves aesthetic quality, the moving image of the cinema fills the spectator with pleasure.

In the obscurity of the cinema hall, the spectator enjoys primal pleasures: the titillation of the moving image, the stirring of emotions, the feeling of togetherness with other spectators in a community of enjoyment, the freedom to laugh at what one would normally find serious, the freedom to go along with the violence perpetrated on the screen in the dim knowledge that nothing actually happens, the freedom of breaking every possible taboo with total impunity and so on.These pleasures are very real. And, notwithstanding Münsterberg's delight in the artistic pleasure furnished by the film, it is the primal pleasures that account for the immense popularity of the cinema.

Not a few spectators are satisfied with these primal pleasures. Yet, quite a few also experience the aesthetic pleasures which films offer. These aesthetic pleasures do not suppress the more basic pleasures, they are of another order. Both orders of pleasure can be subsumed by the same person while watching a film. In the film *Amadeus* Mozart is credited with saying: "I am vulgar, but my art is not vulgar." Film as such is vulgar, but it often elevates the mind to the level of art.

Television has been nicknamed the "idiot box". That is striking, because most people who have access to a teevee set readily give the best hours of their daily life to television. Contrary to cinema which used to be shown in a place set apart especially for it, television constitutes an important part of our domestic environment. Why call teevee idiot when we stare at it for hours? It is our antenna on the world, our faithful companion in loneliness, our encyclopedia, our court jester, our family priest, our doctor, our personal advisor, etc. And it's fun to watch it.

But the pleasure emteevee offers in a sort of frenzy is a vague euphoria, which at times is not without disturbing elements of fear, anxiety, insecurity. On the surface, everything seems happy, but the random avalanche of symbols, the staccato presentation, constantly short-circuit the very possibility of dealing with the images and sounds rationally. Television massages the subconscious part of our minds.

When you saw a film like *Psycho*, you knew that your subconscious was being manipulated. You knew what sorts of feelings were aroused by the film, although you had little idea about the particular mechanisms that were at play, perhaps the tension created by Hitchcock about gender identity, for instance.[12]

But while watching television, why is it that you feel good (I do not say happy) and at the same time vaguely disturbed? A plausible answer to this question is that as a cultural form emteevee corresponds to the present economic stage of late capitalism, that of multinational capital. The so-called "liberalisation" of market regulations, after the stringent "structural adjustments" are symptomatic of an effervescence of the market. Cinema, on the other hand, was the cultural form of monopoly market in the era of colonialism and empire.

There is a definite tendency towards what might be called "immateriality" in television as well as in the present economic order. On the one hand, the owners of capital are not particular, identifiable, persons. They are huge anonymous organisations that are located nowhere in particular or, if you wish, that are everywhere all at once. On the other hand, the products from which profit is derived are more and more immaterial. It is not for nothing that so much is made of "intellectual" property. A nice name to designate trade marks. It is well known to consumers that the trade mark of a successful product is more important than the product itself, and fetches more profit. Add to trade marks, designs, patents, and, above all, copyrights.

These two aspects of immateriality have a great impact on the media scene. For instance, television has put the human body in crisis. Cinema had emphasized the female body and had schooled audiences to gaze with desire at the female body. The body was de-personalised, made into an object. In television humans tend to be at once de-personalised and disembodied. Lacking the sense of depth which cinema had accustomed us to, humans seem to float on the screen. Not unlike astronauts once freed from the law of gravity.

Unfortunately, the debate about the culture of imported programmes[13] misses the essential. The so-called international culture some critics object to is not just a culture among others, an optional culture. It is the necessary culture of multinational capital. Our discomfort in front of the teevee screen is an index of our discomfort with and in the present world economic situation. In all this, we confusedly sense that the media are a celebration of a social order which, as far as we are concerned, appears to be inevitable. But we hesitate to join in the celebration because we somehow know that we would end up celebrating our own subjection to new forms of imperialism and colonialism.

## 5. FILM-MAKERS AND TELEVISION

So far, I have dealt with cinema and television from the point of view of the spectator or viewer. Yet, it is with film-makers that television has had a close encounter of a strange kind. In India the encounter of cinema and television has not been a happy one. It is as if television were a "rakkshash" devouring cinema. Television uses cinema stars, it rehashes film songs, it employs film-makers to produce teevee serials. Meanwhile, films are available on video tapes for home viewing. The end of cinema, it seems, is upon us.[14] We need not be that pessimistic.

As a means of expression, television has not yet developed fully in India. And, therefore, television devours films much in the same way as cinema itself devoured dramas. Cinema does not need television any more than theatre needed cinema. For, both cinema and theatre are complete art forms. Since television has not grown into its own as yet, it needs cinema films. But it can be anticipated that this will last but a few years. Television is a marvellous medium, and when it develops fully it will not need cinema films any more. In fact, it is not television that has not developed, it is the teevee-makers who haven't.

There has first been on the part of film-makers a reaction similar to that of playwrights with regard to cinema. Film-makers were happy to have their films shown on television. Afterwards they were happy to be given assignments by and for television. But they very soon discovered that television destroyed films as films in many ways. First of all the ambience in which a film is seen on the teevee screen does not permit the viewer to watch it attentively. Nor can the viewers at home ordinarily spend nearly two hours at a stretch watching a film. They often miss the beginning, they cannot always watch a film till the end. But it is the very image of a film which suffers when shown on the teevee screen. Some psychologists have claimed that the very teevee image with millions of luminous points damages the viewer's nervous system.

Be that as it may, from the point of view of the spectator, a film on teevee is better than nothing. But from the point of view of the cineaste, the screen rendering of a film is less than nothing, since the film is destroyed. The smallness of the screen is, of course, the first problem: on teevee the film image looses its impact. Moreover, the sharpness, the fine tones one can now produce on the cinema screen are lost on the teevee screen. But what is still more damageable to the film itself is that on fully commercialised television the film is used as the carrier of advertisements.

It is perhaps Jean-Luc Godard who has had the harshest words about the relationship of television and cinema. He said (or did he write? one is never quite sure in his case!): "The birth of television has ruined all the cinemas of Europe."[15]

In despair, film-makers stopped showing their films on television and attempted to make films for television. Some succeeded, others failed. Those who succeeded won over television but they lost cinema. That is because for television you can make television films only, you cannot make cinema films. The relationship between film-makers and television can again be compared with the relationship between people from the theatre and cinema. Orson Welles and Laurence Olivier, for instance, did make excellent films, not filmed dramas. They even extended, especially in the case of Welles, the expressive power of cinema language. But they succeeded, not because they were theatre persons, but because they were artists who, sensitive to the specificity of cinema, developed its potential. We can expect the same to happen with television. Some film-makers will make excellent television films, but not as film-makers. They will do it as television film-makers. (Is it not striking that there is as yet no term for what should be a "teevee maker"!)

For a film-maker, to adjust to the television requirements is suicidal.

## NOTES AND REFERENCES

1. That was the time when Jean-Paul Sartres asked, "what is literature?" and in a rejoinder to Sartres, Barthes asked, "what is writing?"
2. It should be clear enough that there is a diversity of cinemas. Yet, even in his scholarly book, *Language and Cinema* (The Hague: Mouton, 1974) Christian Metz has had to remind his readers of this basic fact. He opens his book with the following lines:

   "What is referred to globally as 'cinema'... is, in reality, a vast and complex socio-cultural phenomenon... which, if taken as a whole, does not lend itself to any rigorous and unified study, but only to a heteroclite collection of observations involving multiple and diverse points of view (plurality of criteria of relevancy)" (p. 9). Quoted by Brian Lewis in Jean Mitry, p. 9.

3. Programmes where listeners can ask questions by phone are offered occasionally by the Indira Gandhi National Open University (IGNOU) and the University Grants Commission's *The Countrywide Classroom*.
4. In theatre everything has to be arranged for a spectator sitting in front of the stage. The image is created with that in mind. But the cinema image is not created for a spectator occupying a fixed position. The cinema image is freed from that single point of view. And the action evolves freely without paying attention, as it were, to the spectator. At every moment the camera is placed wherever it can get the best view of the action. Or, wherever it will get the view the director wants to give to the audience. In the first sequence of *Charulata*, which happens to be a remarkable film rendering of a few pages from a novel, several shots have been conceived theatrically. For instance, when Charu moves from one room to another, she is seen entering the other room from a position similar to that of a theatre spectator, as if the camera was waiting there, like a theatre spectator taking his seat before the curtain rises. In spite of the marvellous photography, the film has in that sequence a high coefficient of theatricality. On the other hand, in the "Kulfee" sequence the film achieves the highest cinematic quality. In teevee serials you often see the actors in groups of two or three facing the television camera as if they were on the stage. As a result, the actors occupy the most unlikely positions with respect to each other, and they look in the most unlikely directions.
5. Münsterberg, a German immigrant, was a pacifist just as the USA entered the war against Germany.
6. Mitry came to know of Münsterberg probably through Brian Lewis who was in Montréal at the time when Mitry taught film at the Université de Montréal. Lewis affirms that at the time of writing his *Esthétique* ... Mitry did not know of *The Photoplay*. In his last book *La Semiologie en Question, langage et cinéma* (Les Editions du Cerf, 1987), Mitry deals with Münsterberg in one line (p. 21). See Brian Lewis, *Jean Mitry and The Aesthetics of the Cinema* (Ann Arbor, Umi Research Press, 1984), p. 17: "*The Photoplay* ... is one of the few theoretical works on film in French or English of which Jean Mitry was not at all aware when he wrote *Esthétique*."

   Mitry, Jean, *Esthétique et psychologie du cinéma*,
   I. *Les structures*, Paris: Editions Universitaires, 1963.
   II. *Les formes*, 1965.
   A shorter version of these two books was prepared by Benoit Patar mostly under Mitry's direction.

Mitry, Jean, *Esthétique et psychologie du cinéma*, Paris: Editions Universitaires, 1990.

Strangely, even today there are scholars who would dismiss Münsterberg. For instance, concluding his essay 'Film/Mind Analogies: the case of Hugo Münsterberg', Noel Carroll (Theorizing the Moving Image, Cambridge University Press, 1996, p. 303) had these lines: 'perhaps what is best learned from his (Münsterberg) effort now is that this line of inquiry should be jettisoned.' In my view, film theory is so poor that it cannot afford to jettison any thing if that thing can be of any use.

The film/mind analogy is criticised as sterile from a theoretical point of view. The main objection being that since we know so little about the processes of the mind, we cannot hope to enlighten film by comparing it with these processes. It is true that we know little about the mind, but we do know something and that much can be useful. Furthermore, there is nothing surprising in the assertion that a film reproduces mind processes. A film is a manner of perceiving, of thinking, and in most cases of narrating. Films, therefore, cannot but be made according to mind processes. If films were not made in that way, spectators could not make sense of them.

The film/mind analogy may not provide the hoped-for foundation of a film theory, but it does prove extremely useful to gain a better understanding of most films, from 'auteur' films to the most popular 'commercial' films. I, for one, would readily jettison the approach if I knew of a more useful one.

7. *What is Cinema?* I, p. 106. See *The Ways of Film Studies*, p. 29.
8. Morin, Edgar, *Le cinéma ou L'homme imaginaire—Cinema or imaginary man*, Paris: Editions de Minuit, 1956. *Chitra Bani*, p. 109.
9. *Chitra Bani*, p. 83; *Sight and Sound*, Summer 1958, p. 240.
10. Jameson, Frederic, *Postmodernism or, The Cultural Logic of Late Capitalism*, London: Verso, 1991, Ch. I, pp. 1-54.
11. Sobchack, Vivian, "The Scene of the Screen: Envisioning Cinematic and Electronic 'Presence'", in Hans Ulrich Gumbrecht and K. Ludwig Pfeiffer, *Materialities of Communication*, Stanford University Press, 1994, pp. 83-106.
12. An interesting analysis of the phenomenon is presented by Linda Williams in her article, "Learning to Scream", in *Sight and Sound*, December 1994, pp. 14-17.
13. It does not matter if the programmes are manufactured in India since they are made according to the same aesthetics.
14. A paraphrase of Abel Gance's ecstatic piece: "The time of the image is upon us". See my *Chitra Bani*, p. 128.
15. Bellour, Raymond, and Mary Lea Bandy, eds., *Jean-Luc Godard, Son+Image 1974-91*, New York: The Museum of Modern Art, 1992.

# ENVOI

# 38. From Morosity to Hope

The media of communication keep giving us the news of disasters happening the world over. So much so that a person who watches the television, for instance, a few hours a day is literally immersed in an environment of murders, wars, violence of every sort, and dishonesty.... That is not all that the media, and television in particular, give the media consumer, but it is a good part of what they offer. The media develop in us an acute awareness of the corruption—a theologian would say of sin—prevalent in the world. But besides the 'news' that we get from the media it is only too easy to observe around us a corruption which seems to overcome body and soul.

In the midst of corruption, both moral and physical, it is imperative to nurture hope. Corruption is the process whereby the quality of life deteriorates. Hope is the thrust of life towards fullness. Any attitude, action, project which is not hopeful leads to morosity, the condition of those who do not see why one should hope but do not have the courage to despair.

It may be that most of us live through periods of morosity. That condition, then, is almost normal, so long as one does not tarry in it. For, indeed, it is not easy to hope. There is, of course, a God-given hope which is selectively blind, as it were, that is, blind to certain facts, and yet is illumined with a vision, a utopia. But I am speaking here mainly of human hope. And human hope is a choice and a commitment.

Over a century ago, prince Kropotkin, the Russian revolutionary anarchist, wrote that "it is hope, not despair, which makes successful revolutions". There is no doubt that the winners in the current international game will be people of hope.

In the middle of the nineteen nineties one observes that the quality of life has deteriorated. There are disturbing signs all around: more people are sick than before, and even new illnesses have appeared; more people than before are jobless; there are more illiterates; more people are poor even though the rich grow richer. But that increase in misfortune is largely due to the fact that today there are far more people on earth than there used to be. And the old systems that in the past cared for vast populations now prove inadequate. One fact, however, has to be noted: there are systems that seem to cause of necessity the misfortune of the majority of the people on earth. On the other hand, there are other systems which, without being perfect, seem more capable to foster the welfare of the majority.

On the other hand, there are positive signs too: apart from the hysteria it provoked, the 1994 outburst of the plague in India has left a relatively small number of victims in comparison with the devastation it wrought in so many countries just a few decades ago. The positive element of this latter example has not always been emphasized by the media. It was there to be seen, none the less.

Other positive signs are obvious: rural people, that is, half the population of the world, have access to many more goods than they used to. They have access to much more information than before due to the spread of radio and television. The day when there is a functioning phone in every village of India, for instance, is not far off. Even now, people from distant villages can communicate more easily than before. They can phone to a relative who has migrated abroad or who is working there, and that relative too can phone back home.

Not a few people above fifty years of age today have personally experienced a significant rise in the quality of their lives and they would not wish to go back to the somewhat primitive ways of their youth. But worldwide, how many people above fifty feel that way?

Our minds too have changed over the last few decades. Nearly a century of Marxism has reminded us of the importance of economics in the life of both individuals and societies. One might not have needed Marxism to realise that the exchange of goods is essential to human life. As a matter of fact, though, we did learn a lot from Marx's thought.

On the other hand, socialism—of whatever type—has taught us that the exchange of goods cannot be centrally regulated. The possession of goods cannot be vested in the state, and we have to achieve a balance between total anarchy (the free market idea?) and total control. Unfortunately, the great media are in the service of the dominating ideology, and they dismiss socialism somewhat hurriedly and in an only too obviously motivated manner.

Today the production of goods and services is rarely designed to meet the requirements of rural people the world over. The great corporations across national borders and the great companies within countries rarely consider the needs of the rural folks because they do not envisage these people as eventual consumers of goods. But rural people nonetheless potentially constitute the largest and most homogeneous market of the world. If they do not buy the products of the transnationals, it is often because these goods are not designed to meet their pressing needs. Yet, in India, at least, the great companies have started to perceive the purchasing potential of the farmers. Accordingly, they have adjusted their strategies not only in the marketing but also in the design of their products.

There is a feeling that rural folks are slow to change their ways. Anthropologists tell us that that is not the case. After all, a rural person has to earn a living from his work, and he is on the lookout for opportunities to improve his lot. He may not readily take risks. But he sees what can be useful and gainful for him and his family. Evidently, he too can be easy prey to a publicity contered on consumption.

It should be clear too that narrow nationalism has no survival value. What has value is one's identity and culture. The state is not able any more to protect and nurture these. Moreover, these characteristics, which constitute the wealth of the human family, can be protected only by the individuals concerned. Values disappear when no one bothers to nurture them. They are not slaughtered from outside. As long as one cares for one's language, for instance, it will endure. But the cultivation of one's language is not done by closing the door to other languages. Unfortunately, there is a form of militantism for which the defense of some values must be done "against" some other values. That does not work. One does not develop one's language, for instance, by fighting against another language. It is true that at times steps must be taken against other languages and values, but the thrust of one's effort is not "against" others, but "in favour" of one's own values.

The great debates prompted by nationalisms are a choiced material for the communication media. But these debates often divert the attention of people if not from their real problems at least from the real causes of their problems. Media consumers raely have the time to think over all the stories they are told. And, willy-nilly, they are often carried away by the tide. Yet, it is absolutely necessary to anchor oneself, to stop and raise fundamental questions. Is it true, for instance, that there is no sustainable alternative to the world as we know it? Are we helplessly delivered to the power of the consumption ideology. In order to dare ask these questions, you already need the hope that they can be answered favourably.

Hope is a choice. Morosity too is a choice: a choice often prompted by laziness, turpitude, morbidity. Above all morosity is a sort of moral anemia. Physical anemia is a condition in which the quality of the blood of an individual person is poor and, as a result, the individual is weak. The metaphor is apt. Morosity is anemia.

What we need today is a set of energetic ideas and images along with positive examples and pragmatic plans to strengthen us and help us all to move decidedly from morosity to hope. It is perhaps time we gave anew to the media, and hence to the persons who direct them, the certainty that, after all, the media themselves can create hope.

## REFERENCES

Roberge, Gaston, *Mediation, the action of the media in our society*, New Delhi: Manohar, 1978.

"What Can Multinationals Do for Peasants", *Studies in Third World Societies*, No. 49, Feb. 1994, Department of Anthropology, College of William and Mary, Williamsburg, Virginia.

# Name Index